Languedoc

Intelligent Guides to Wines & Top Vineyards

Benjamin Lewin MW

Copyright © 2015 Benjamin Lewin

Ver 1.11 08-16

Vendange Press

www.vendangepress.com

Preface

Based on my book, *Wines of France*, this Guide is devoted specifically to Languedoc. The first part discusses the region and its wines; the second part has individual profiles of the top producers. The basic idea is that the first part explains the character and range of the wines, and the second part shows how each winemaker interprets that character.

In the first part I address the nature of the wines made today and ask how this has changed, how it's driven by tradition or competition, and how styles may evolve in the future. I show how the wines are related to the terroir and to the types of grape varieties that are grown, and I explain the classification system. For each region, I suggest reference wines that I believe typify the area; in some cases, where there is a split between, for example, modernists and traditionalists, there may be wines from each camp.

There's no single definition for what constitutes a top producer. Leading producers range from those who are so prominent as to represent the common public face of an appellation to those who demonstrate an unexpected potential on a tiny scale. The producers profiled in the guide should represent the best of both tradition and innovation in wine in the region

In the profiles, I have tried to give a sense of each producer's aims for his wines, of the personality and philosophy behind them— to meet the person who makes the wine, as it were, as much as to review the wines themselves. For each producer I suggest reference wines that are a good starting point for understanding his style. Most of the producers welcome visits, although some require appointments: details are in the profiles.

The guide is based on many visits to France over recent years. I owe an enormous debt to the hundreds of producers who cooperated in this venture by engaging in discussion and opening innumerable bottles for tasting. This guide would not have been possible without them.

Benjamin Lewin

How to read the producer profiles

The second part of this guide consists of profiles of individual wine producers. Each profile shows a sample label, a picture of the winery, and details of production, followed by a description of the producer and winemaker. The producer's rating (from one to four stars) is shown to the right of the name.

The profiles are organized geographically, and each group of profiles is preceded by a map showing the locations of starred producers to help plan itineraries.

A full list of the symbols used in the profiles appears at the start of the profile section. This is an example of a profile:

Hospices de Beaune

Hospices de Beaune

Hotel Dieu, Beaune, France
address

03 80 24 44 02

Catherine Guillemot

catherine.guillemot@ch-beaune.fr

Corton *principal AOP*

Beaune 1er, Nicolas Rolin
red reference wine

Corton Charlemagne, Charlotte Dumay
white reference wine

www.hospices-de-beaune.com

details of producer
60 ha; 400,000 bottles
vineyards & production

The Hospices de Beaune was founded in 1443 by Nicolas Rolin, chancellor of Burgundy, as a hospital for the poor. Standing in the heart of Beaune, the original buildings of the Hotel Dieu, now converted into a museum, surround a courtyard where an annual auction of wines was first held in 1859. The wines come from vineyards held as part of the endowment of the Hospices, and are sold in November to negociants who then take possession of the barrels and mature the wines in their own styles. (Today the auction is held in the modern covered marketplace opposite the Hotel Dieu.) There are 45 cuvées (32 red and 13 white); most come from premier or grand crus from the Côte de Beaune or Côte de Nuits, but because holdings are small (depending on past donations of land to the Hospices) many cuvées consist of blends from different crus (and are identified by brand names). The vines are cultivated, and the wine is made, by the Hospices. For some years the vineyards of the Hospices were not tended as carefully as they might have been, and the winemaking was less than perfect, but the appointment of a new régisseur has led to improvements in the present century. The name of the Hospices is only a starting point, because each negociant stamps his own style on the barriques he buys.

Contents

The Languedoc

Goes to my head...
Red, red wine
Stay close to me
(UB40)

If the Languedoc were an independent country, it would be in fifth place in the world for wine production (more or less equal with Argentina and after the United States). It accounts for one third of all wine production in France. To give it its full name, Languedoc-Roussillon is a vast area, stretching around the Mediterranean from near the Rhône to the Pyrenees at the west. (Roussillon is the southernmost part adjacent to Spain). To say that the history of wine production is chequered would be kind. Together with Provence, immediately to its east, the region used to be known as the Midi, famous for providing the major bulk of Europe's wine lake, a vast quantity of characterless wine from high-yielding varieties. But things are different today. Overall production has decreased sharply, production of Vin de Table has been reduced to a small proportion, and although production remains predominantly IGP, there are some AOPs establishing good reputations. Most of the wine is red.

Rich is the word that comes most immediately to mind to describe the style. The warm climate makes this a fertile area for growing grapes, but until recently, quantity ruled over quality. At the start of the nineteenth century, the focus was on producing wine for distillation; the Languedoc made about 40% of all spirits in France. After the railway connected Montpellier to Paris in 1845, producers switched to making cheap table wine that could be sent to the industrial cities in the north. Phylloxera wiped out the vineyards here as elsewhere—there were riots in Montpellier in 1907 to protest cheap imports of wine from Algeria—but by the second decade of the twentieth century, recovery was under way. Production still focused on price; wine was produced as cheaply as possible, often blended with foreign imports, and sold in bulk. Almost all was Vin de Table, and as the demand for plonk declined, this surplus became the largest single contributor to Europe's wine

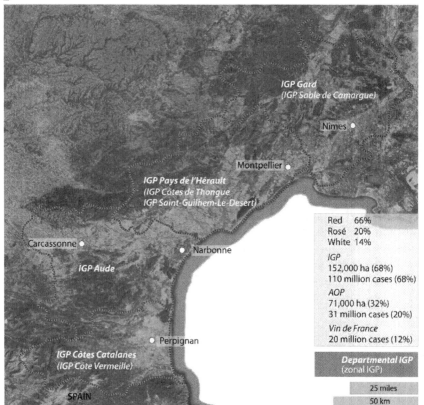

IGP Gard
(IGP Sable de Camargue)

Nîmes ●

Montpellier ●

IGP Pays de l'Hérault
(IGP Côtes de Thongue
IGP Saint-Guilhem-Le-Desert)

Carcassonne ●

● Narbonne

IGP Aude

Red	66%
Rosé	20%
White	14%

IGP
152,000 ha (68%)
110 million cases (68%)

AOP
71,000 ha (32%)
31 million cases (20%)

Vin de France
20 million cases (12%)

○ Perpignan

IGP Côtes Catalanes
(IGP Côte Vermeille)

Departmental IGP
(zonal IGP)

25 miles
50 km

SPAIN

Languedoc-Roussillon stretches from Nîmes to the Spanish border. The IGP d'Oc covers the whole area, and includes four departmental IGPs. IGP Côtes Catalanes corresponds to Roussillon; IGP Aude and IGP Pays d'Hérault are the heart of Languedoc; and IGP Gard extends from the Languedoc into the Rhône. Some of the better known zonal IGPs are named in parentheses.

lake. At its peak around 1970, Languedoc-Roussillon had 450,000 hectares of vineyards.

Economic difficulties, combined with incentives to abandon production, led to a substantial decline in vineyard areas. Over the past forty years, production has declined by about half. In fact, subsidies for pulling up vineyards became a significant part of the income of the Languedoc. Today there are about 220,000 hectares of vineyards. The number of growers has declined, and in spite of a move by the more enterprising to bottle their own wine, the cooperatives are more important here than anywhere else in France. Of the 700 cooperatives in France, around 500 are in the Languedoc, where the struggle of the past twenty years has been to improve quality. Overall, 72% of production goes through coops.

The decline in production has been accompanied by a move to quality. The major change has come in the collapse of Vin de Table production, now only about 10% of its peak, and alone responsible for most of the decline in the category in France. Even so, almost half of France's remaining Vin de Table (now named Vin de France) still comes from the Languedoc. IGP has increased about three fold; the Languedoc is now far and way France's most important producer of wine at the IGP level. Of course, the change is partly cosmetic: the vast increase in IGP has come from vineyards that used to be Vin de Table.

Accounting for more than three quarters of production, the IGP Pays d'Oc covers the whole region, and is the prominent face of the Languedoc. Within the generic IGP are four Départemental IGPs: IGP de Gard, IGP Pays d'Hérault, IGP d'Aude, and IGP Côtes Catalanes (the last represents the Pyrénées-Oriéntal département, effectively equivalent to Roussillon). There are also many zonal IGPs, varying from single communes to broader swatches of the area, but almost none has established any typicity or made any particular reputation. Many grape varieties are allowed in the IGPs, and wines can be monovarietal, blended from two varieties, or blended from multiple varieties. Under the old system, there was an attempt to identify a better class of Vin de Pays with the introduction of the Grand d'Oc classification in 2001, intended for no more than a percent of the wines, but this seems to have died with the transition to IGP. It was in any case controversial whether the additional classification fitted with the concept of Vin de Pays.

For several decades the Languedoc was plagued by the characterless wines produced by the infamous trio of Carignan, Cinsault, and Aramon; today these are only a quarter of the black varieties. A major drive to improve quality a few years back focused on "cépage amelioration," the replacement of poor quality varieties with better ones. Its success is indicated by the fact that Syrah (introduced relatively recently) and Grenache (a traditional variety of the region) overtook Carignan as the most planted varieties in 2009. In fact, there is now more Syrah and Grenache in Languedoc-

Even Vieilles Vignes Carignan produces large bunches.

Roussillon than in the Rhône. The newcomer Merlot is the last of the big four. Cabernet Sauvignon is in a distant fifth place. White varieties are less than a quarter of all plantings, with Chardonnay and Sauvignon Blanc now the leading varieties.

In spite of its evident deficiencies—most notably the tendency to over produce—Carignan remains a major variety. Its history is not encouraging: "Carignan was introduced from Spain and was planted everywhere to make Vin de Table. It eliminated all the traditional cépages," says Jean Orliac at Domaine de l'Hortus. Reality is recognized in the AOP rules by allowing it to be included, but often restricting the maximum proportion. Carignan's tendency to show bitterness without fruitiness is sometimes counteracted by using carbonic maceration (similar to Beaujolais), but the result does not show much typicity. My general marker for a wine made from Carignan, or containing a large proportion of it, is a certain flatness, a lack of liveliness, on the palate.

But because almost no one is planting Carignan any more, what's left tends to be old vines. Some committed producers regard the old Carignan as the glory of the Languedoc. "Carignan is the great classic vine of the Languedoc, it's the Pinot Noir of the

Reference Wines for Vieilles Vignes Carignan	
Faugères	*Château de La Liquière, Nos Racines*
IGP Hauterive (Corbières region)	*Château La Baronne, Pièce de Roche*
IGP du Mont Baudile (Hérault)	*Domaine d'Aupilhac, Le Carignan*
IGP Côtes Catalanes (Roussillon)	*Domaine Olivier Pithon, Le Pilou* *Domaine du Mas Amiel, Val de Nuits* *Domaine Roc Des Anges, Vignes Centenaires Carignan*
Vin de France (Corbières region)	*Domaine Ledogar, La Mariole*
Vin de France (Saint Christol)	*Terre Inconnue, Cuvée Léonie*

Languedoc. Why doesn't it have a better reputation? It's been a victim of its success. It's been planted everywhere, and because it's a productive variety, people have made wine at very high yields. But at low yields it is perfectly adapted to the terroir," says Rémy Pédréno at Roc L'Anglade. My own view is that vines have to be a century old before the wine comes into an elegant balance that lets the fruit become the dominant note. Granted that the fruit profile of Carignan will always be flatter compared with the exuberance of Grenache or the freshness of Syrah, you can certainly find some Vieilles Vignes Carignans that are elegant, smooth, and seamless.

Most IGP wines carry varietal labels; in fact, the Languedoc is the largest source of varietal-labeled wines in France. The order of importance of varietal-labeled wines looks quite different from tradition: Merlot, Cabernet Sauvignon, Syrah, and Chardonnay scarcely existed in the region twenty years ago. By contrast, the AOPs are blended wines, and carry identification only of origin. The generic Languedoc AOP requires a minimum 50% of the GSM trio (Grenache, Syrah, and Mourvèdre) for red or rosé (which in effect means Syrah and Grenache as there is relatively little Mourvèdre). Each individual AOP has its variations on this theme.

Chardonnay and Sauvignon Blanc are not allowed in white AOPs; the use of Viognier is restricted, so it also tends to be found only in the IGPs. Because all of the AOPs in Languedoc require wines to be blended from at least two or three grape varieties, producers who want to make monovarietal wines, even from traditional varieties, are forced to declassify them to IGP or even to Vin de France.

It's a major distinction between the IGPs and the AOPs that international varieties are grown in the IGPs, whereas they are mostly not allowed in the AOPs. This means there tends to be a difference in character as well as quality between AOP and IGP, with the AOP more traditional, and the IGP more "international" in the choice of varieties. "In the Midi you can cultivate all the cépages, although their characters may be different from elsewhere. It's really a matter of deciding what type of wine you want to provide," says Serge Martin-Pierrat at Château les Hospitaliers. There is continuing debate as to whether concentrating on making wines from the traditional varieties in the AOPs, or producing international varieties in the IGPs, is the best way forward. There's some criticism of INAO for its insistence on maintaining the original Southern varieties as the exclusive basis for AOP wines.

Modernism elsewhere in France tends to imply a move towards a more "international" style, usually meaning greater extraction to make more powerful wines. In the Languedoc, it has almost the opposite meaning; a move away from the old, heavy, extracted alcoholic styles to finer, more elegant wines (although there will always be alcohol in Languedoc). Innovation at the top level does not so much take the direction of trying new varieties, but more on moving in a more refined direction with the varieties (Grenache, Carignan, Cinsault, and more recently Syrah) that were previously known for producing powerful alcoholic wines. Ageworthiness is becoming an issue. "People have forgotten that wines of the south can age—it's a pity. You can forget about the wine for 8-10 years and then drink it. But people think they need to drink the wines of the south straight away," says Frédéric Pourtalié at Domaine de Montcalmès.

There is definite progress, with excess production diminishing, and plantings of better varieties increasing, but no clear regional leader has emerged. With its (relatively) reliably hot climate, Languedoc-Roussillon better resembles the wine-producing regions of the New World than any other part of France. Today you meet many thoughtful, intelligent winemakers in Languedoc who are rethinking what they can do with the region, the very antithesis of the old view of the Midi as a bulk producer of rustic wines. Many are young winemakers for whom one attraction is that the Languedoc is one of the last places where they can still afford to buy vineyards.

AOP regions make up a third of the area, and AOP production has been reasonably constant at just under a quarter of all volume for several years, but there are continuing changes in the organization of the AOPs. The region was divided into different appellations in the early 1980s, and since then a significant part of the effort to improve wine production in the Languedoc has focused on developing a hierarchy.

Languedoc AOPs

	cases
Languedoc	4,400,000
Corbières	6,200,000
Cabardès	200,000
Faugères	770,000
Limoux	900,000
Malepère	220,200
Minervois	1,700,000
Minervois-Lavinière	77,000
Muscats du Languedoc	420,000
Saint Chinian	1,400,000

Insofar as there is any geographical integrity within such a large region, it falls into three parts. The area from Montpellier to Narbonne used to be covered by a catch-all AOC called Coteaux du Languedoc. This has been replaced by the regional Languedoc AOP, which essentially includes *all* of the AOP areas, all the way from Montpellier to the Spanish border. The stated objective is to "define the typical characteristics of the Languedoc region and grapes," but the creation of such a broad appellation seems retrogressive, since it's really impossible for it to have any coherence. Most of the wines in the Languedoc AOP are the same wines that used to be labeled as Coteaux du

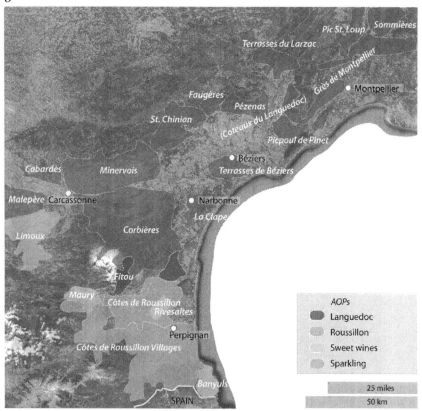

The AOPs of Languedoc-Roussillon extend from Montpellier (west of the Rhône) to the Spanish border.

Languedoc, but there are some from additional areas, and others from within sub-regional AOPs that for one reason or another do not fit the requirements of their particular AOP.

The best parts of the old Coteaux du Languedoc are the new appellations of Pic St. Loup and Terrasses du Larzac. The soil is poor, the sun is hot in summer, there can be dramatic rainstorms off the mountains, and the cold wind from the north dries everything out. Spreading out from the base of Mont Hortus, Pic St. Loup is a plateau surrounded by calcareous cliffs. The AOP of Terrasses de Larzac takes its name from the protective mountains to the north. Cool air coming down from the Larzac plateau creates a microclimate with very high diurnal variation, up to 20 degrees, the highest in Languedoc: "That's what preserves acidity and gives the elegance," says Frédéric Pourtalié at Domaine de Montcalmès. Vineyards are at elevations from 80 m to 200 m on the slopes of two valleys. A tasting of Grenache barrel samples from different terraces in the eastern part of the appellation shows a range from a jammy impression where there are galets (large pebbles), to broad flavors from the calcareous terroir at the base of the slope, to more mineral overtones from vineyards at higher altitude. The wines can be more restrained here (relatively speaking). A little farther west and at lower elevation in Jonquières, Mas Cal Demoura divides its vineyards into those with more clay (planted with black varieties) and the more pebbly and calcareous (planted with white varieties). "Terrasses de Larzac has a balance between traditional generosity of Languedoc with an additional liveliness and freshness," says Vincent Goumard at Cal Demoura. There's enough variation across the AOP to find places that are suitable for each grape variety.

The heart of the Languedoc is a large semicircle of AOPs radiating around Narbonne—the producers' organization likes to talk about the amphitheater of AOPs. Languedoc now includes around thirty AOPs, but the core AOPs are Faugères, St. Chinian, Minervois, Fitou, and Corbières (this last being about the size of all the others combined). The reputations of the appellations really pertain to their red wines: some of them in fact allow only red wine, with the whites labeled simply as Languedoc. INAO refused to allow the Languedoc to have grand crus, but has allowed crus to be delineated within some of the appellations: these are Minervois La Livinière, Corbières Boutenac, St. Chinian Berlou, and St. Chinian Roquebrun.

There is a certain scepticism among producers about the usefulness of a detailed hierarchical classification. "Languedoc is a vast region. It's very heterogeneous. What matters is the quality of the work, rather than the label or the AOP. There are really only twenty or so domains of interest, in my opinion. For me the appellation has no importance, it's the work on the terroir that counts," says Paul Lignères at Château La Baronne in Corbières. There's a feeling that the process has been rushed. "For me arriving at a cru means a high quality, it must really be better. But it takes time to do that. We haven't got the microclimates that Burgundy has. With a young appellation you can't divide into crus in only thirty years, it takes time to know the terroir," says Jean-François

Calcareous cliffs loom over the vineyards of Pic St. Loup.

Orosquette at Château La Grave in Minervois. Nearby at Château La Tour Boisée, Jean-Louis Poudou believes the process is too political. "You can't decree a cru just like that—it's an INAO-esque method that irritates me. There are producers who are increasing the quality of the Languedoc. The organization of crus, for example in the Coteaux du Languedoc, is more of an administrative matter: it's all a political issue. The two appellations that genuinely have independence are St. Chinian and Faugères. There are really only two Crus—La Livinière and Boutenac," he says.

The name "Midi" somehow conjures up an impression of a vast plain of vines, but actually much of the Languedoc is distinctly mountainous. From Pic St. Loup, north of Montpellier, to La Clape just inland from Narbonne, massive calcareous cliffs overlook the vineyards. While it may be difficult to pinpoint characteristics of each area, there are both widespread and local differences. As a rough measure, Syrah is more dominant in the north and Carignan is more dominant in the west, but the common focus across the region on GSM (Grenache-Syrah-Mourvèdre) blends with or without Carignan means that differences between appellations

Faugères has thin topsoil based on a deep layer of schist.

should be due principally to terroir or climatic variations rather than varieties. So how distinctive are the appellations: was the effort in distinguishing them really justified, and are the crus really distinct in character and quality?

Some of the appellations are relatively homogeneous with regards to soil types, while others vary quite extensively, so there is no simple rule. While there are some differences in temperatures and rainfall, depending on proximity to cliffs, elevation of vineyards, and exposure to maritime influence, the fact is that the Languedoc is a warm, dry climate prone to make powerful wines. Skillful winemaking is key in restraining the reds and keeping freshness in the whites: the producer is the most important variable. Faugères was reportedly denied cru status because a large proportion of its production is vinified by the cooperative and sold at prices that are felt to be too low for a cru, but it was considered one of the more promising appellations when the AOCs were first established. The day I visited Faugères was autumnal, a week or so after the harvest. The road to Faugères climbs up steadily for miles, and by the time we arrived, the vineyards on the slopes were shrouded in a mist so thick you could scarcely see from vine to vine. Faugères seemed to be floating in the clouds. Terroir is based on very friable grey schist, typically 6-7 m deep. It's relatively homogeneous, divided between grey and violet schist. How is this reflected in the wine?

A tasting at Jean-Michel Alquier, one of the leading producers, showed wines in a variety of styles: fresh and light for La Première, the GSM entry level wine from the base of the slope; fruity with a touch of piquancy for Maison Jaune, a Grenache-dominated wine from the middle of the slope; and massive black fruits for Le Bastide, a Syrah-dominated wine from the top of the hill, developing very slowly indeed over a decade. The distinguishing feature isn't merely the producer, but winemaking choices along the way. "There was a period when everyone used new wood and the wines tended to taste the same, but now we have taken a step back," explains Jean-Michel.

There's a similar philosophy and range at Château de La Liquière. "At the start of the 2000s, people were trying to make wines that were very powerful. In Languedoc it's very easy to make wines that are very powerful. But public taste began to change and vignerons realized that great concentration reduces expression of terroir. People started to use less aggressive methods, including short maceration," says winemaker François Vidal. The entry level wine, Les Amandiers, classified as Languedoc, comes from the vines at lower elevation, while Cistus, the top Faugères, comes from vines higher up. "It's generally true—for both reds and whites—that more complexity and elegance, length and finesse, come from vines at high altitudes," says François. So in this sense the top wines are wines of altitude.

Adjacent to Faugères, Saint Chinian is sometimes said to make harder wines than Faugères. It is divided in two by the rivers Orb and Vernazobre. To the north, the vein of schist extends from Faugères, mixed with subsoil of grès (gravelly marl, a sort of muddy limestone). The vineyards in this part of the appellation are on the hills, whereas those in the south are on the plain below, where the soil is calcareous with clay. There's a view that wines coming from schist are more mineral, whereas those from the clay-chalk soils of the south are firmer. The two crus, Berlou and Roquebrun, occupy scattered areas in the north, with soils marked by schist, and an interesting difference in their grape varieties: Roquebrun must have less than 30% Carignan, whereas Berlou has a minimum of 30% Carignan. A series of cuvées from different terroirs produced by Jean-François Izarn at Borie La Vitarèle shows more obvious structure in Les Schistes, coming from terroir like Faugères, and more rounded, forceful fruits, in Les Crès, coming from terroir with round galet pebbles that resembles Châteauneuf-du-Pape.

A relatively large area to the east of the ancient city of Carcassonne, Minervois has different terroirs. Soil types, elevations, and climatic exposure are quite varied, including the characteristic grès, as well as calcareous soils, schists, marble, and large pebbles. This makes it hard to get a bead on typicity. In the north of the appellation, the cru of La Lavinière has 200 ha of vineyards; this represents only some 5% of Minervois, and is restricted to red wines at slightly lower yields than Minervois. Even in this restricted area, there is significant heterogeneity, a sort of recapitulation in miniature of the entire area of Minervois. The tendency in Minervois is to make cuvées from different terroirs, giving interesting variety, but making it difficult to define any single character for the appellation. At the northeast corner of Minervois, Saint-Jean-de-Minervois is a small appellation focused on fortified sweet wines.

If Minervois is heterogeneous, then Corbières, adjacent and much larger, can verge on incoherence. A major part of production goes to negociants or cooperatives (where the giant Val d'Orbieu cooperative is predominant). The result is that only a small proportion of Corbières is actually bottled by growers. Corbières-Boutenac is the cru, characterized by a good proportion of very old Carignan vines (often dating back more than a century). Here the proportion of Syrah is limited to 30%, so if there is anywhere that will make the case for Carignan, this is it. Carved out of the southern end of Corbières, Fitou consists of two completely separated areas. It's not obvious why it's a separate appellation as opposed to a cru of Corbières.

It may be difficult for the outsider to obtain a clear bead on Corbières, but the AOP has a firm view of its typicity, or rather, of what isn't its typicity. A producer of natural wines, Domaine Ledogar has a mix of wines in the AOP and Vin de France. "All my

Corbières is hilly and rugged. Courtesy Jean-Luc Raby.

parcels are in Corbières-Boutenac, I present my wines for approval because I was born here, but some do not conform. Why? Because I don't add yeast, I don't add tannins, I don't acidify... so my wines don't conform! They are true wines of terroir" says Xavier Ledogar. "And because Corbières must be a blend, I don't present my monocépages." La Mariole is a cuvée from century-old Carignan; precise and refined, it is the very model of a modern Languedoc. Tout Nature is a classic blend showing the broader flavors of what you might call old Languedoc, but that did not get approval to be labeled as Corbières. So here are two of the best wines of the appellation, respectively representing more modern and traditional styles, which in fact are labeled as Vin de France without any indication that they come from Corbières!

To the east of Corbières, La Clape is a relatively small AOP, but somewhat varied. Inland, it seems more like the appellations at the northern extremes of Languedoc: massive calcareous cliffs loom over the area. This is the driest part of Languedoc—it rains less then forty days per year—but the climate is softened by the humidity resulting from proximity to the sea. By the coast vineyards run down almost to the water. Styles vary across the appellation.

At the western boundary of Languedoc, the appellations are a little different. Just north of Carcassonne, the small appellations of Malepère and Cabardès have just enough exposure to the Atlantic climate to be allowed to include the Bordelais varieties (Merlot, Cabernet Sauvignon, and Cabernet Franc), not to mention Malbec and Fer Servadou, as well as Syrah and Grenache. The best wines here are based on combinations of Syrah and Cabernet Sauvignon. Just to the south is Limoux, where the focus is on sparkling wines, with the traditional Blanquette now giving way to the more modern Crémant.

IGPs: d'Oc & Hérault

IGP d'Oc	million cases
Production :	65.0
Varietals :	55.0
Merlot :	16.5
Cabernet Sauvignon :	11.0
Chardonnay :	6.7
Syrah :	4.7
Sauvignon Blanc :	3.8
Grenache :	1.3
Viognier :	1.1

The label of IGP d'Oc is by far and away the single largest category of wine in France, accounting for two thirds of all IGP production and 90% of all varietal-labeled wines. It represents a third of all vineyards in the Languedoc. Altogether 56 varieties are authorized in IGP d'Oc, but two thirds of production is represented by varietal wines coming from only five international varieties. Brands from large negociants (and cooperatives) are a significant proportion of production.

Within the four departments included in the region, the Hérault is the most important, essentially providing the engine of the Languedoc. With more than 90,000 hectares of plantings (three quarters in IGP), its vineyards make it the second most important department in France for wine production. (The Gironde is first, with just over 100,000 ha in Bordeaux.) The Hérault accounts for more than a third of wine

Reference Wines for Red Languedoc	
(Coteaux du) Languedoc	*Prieuré St. Jean de Bébian* *Domaine Peyre Rose, Clos Léone*
Corbières	*Domaine Ledogar, Tout Natur (Vin de France)*
Faugères	*Jean-Michel Alquier, La Maison Jaune* *Château de La Liquière, Cistus*
La Clape	*Château De Pech Redon, Centaurée*
Languedoc-Montpeyroux	*Domaine d'Aupilhac*
Languedoc-Pézenas	*Domaine les Aurelles, Solen*
Minervois	*Château La Tour Boisée, Marie-Claude*
Pic St. Loup	*Domaine de L'Hortus, Grand Cuvée* *Clos Marie, Metairies du Clos*
Saint Chinian	*Borie La Vitarèle, Les Crès*
Terrasses du Larzac	*Mas Cal Demoura, Feu Sacré* *Mas Jullien, Carlan*
IGP de Gard	*Roc d'Anglade*
IGP Pays d'Hérault	*Mas de Daumas Gassac* *Domaine de la Grange des Pères* *Domaine d'Aupilhac, Les Plôs de Baumes*

produced in the Languedoc, and after the catch-all IGP d'Oc, the IGP Pays d'Hérault is the best known of the region's IGPs.

The Hérault is also home to some of the top wines of the Languedoc; denied AOP status because they do not conform to the rules for varietal blending, these are simply labeled as IGP Pays d'Hérault. Just to the west of Montpellier, Aniane is home to two of the producers, Mas de Daumas Gassac and Domaine de la Grange des Pères, who completely defied tradition in the area when they created their wines.

The pioneer for Cabernet Sauvignon in the Languedoc was Mas de Daumas Gassac, where winemaking began in 1972 as the result of an accidental encounter. Aimé Guibert had bought a house and land at Aniane, near Montpellier, as a country residence. The family was considering what sort of agricultural use they might find for the land when a family friend, the famous geographer Henri Enjalbert, remarked during a visit that the terroir reminded him of Burgundy's Côte d'Or and would make a remarkable vineyard. Aniane is a special place, not only for its red glacial soils, but also for the protected microclimate in the Gassac Valley, where cool night winds give greater diurnal variation than elsewhere in the vicinity.

The Guiberts were not much impressed with the local grape varieties. They did not feel that the climate was right for Pinot Noir, and as Bordeaux drinkers they naturally gravitated towards Cabernet Sauvignon. As Aimé recounts, "I consulted all the great oracles in Languedoc, asking them, 'How do you make great wine?' And these great professionals invariably answered, 'If it were possible to make great wine in Languedoc, we would already know about it.' They made fun of me." But by 1978, Emile Peynaud, the doyen of Bordeaux oenologists, became an advisor, and Mas de Daumas Gassac produced its first vintage, a blend based on Cabernet Sauvignon.

The blend has changed over the years, but has generally consisted of around 80% Cabernet Sauvignon with the remainder coming from a wide range of varieties, some Bordelais, others more exotic: initially they were mostly Malbec, Tannat, Merlot, and Syrah; by 1990 they were described as Cabernet Franc, Syrah and Merlot; and today the label just says "several other varieties." One reason for adjusting the blend may have been to calm down the tannins, as some criticism had been expressed of rustic tannins, and current winemaker Samuel Guibert says freely that the wines could be tough and tight for the first few years. In the mid nineties, the young wines started to show more elegance and finesse, he says, probably as a result of increasing vine age.

The avowed intention is to produce a "grand cru" of the Languedoc, but these are not always obvious wines to characterize in the context of Cabernet Sauvignon. "We don't make a Cabernet wine; we make Daumas Gassac. The wine is no more typical of Bordeaux than it is of Languedoc," Samuel says. Perhaps the character of the wine depends on whether Atlantic or Mediterranean influences predominate during the vintage. I find something of a split, with some vintages tending more towards the savory, which I see as Atlantic influence, while others are softer and less obviously structured, which is more what you might expect of the Mediterranean. The differences for me really amplify with age, and were typified by the 1982 and 1983 vintages, the former tending more towards classic savory characteristics of Bordeaux, the latter more towards the soft, perfumed quality of the south. Cabernet is more obvious in the Atlantic vintages; it can be more difficult to perceive in some Mediterranean vintages. Today's wines may be more elegant, with notes of the garrigue cutting the black fruits of the palate, but perhaps they are not so long lived as those from the eighties.

At Daumas Gassac they tried the traditional local varieties of Carignan, Grenache, and Syrah for a while, but eventually pulled them out because they seemed to over-produce and lack finesse in this terroir. Almost adjacent, however, is the Domaine de la Grange des Pères, where the philosophy is almost the antithesis, but the wines are equally interesting. Laurent Vaillé established Grange des Pères soon after Daumas Gassac; his first vintage was 1982. It's not especially easy to make an appointment with Laurent who is nothing if not reticent, but the rendezvous, if successful, takes place in the working cave, where samples can be tasted from barriques. The wine is a blend of roughly equal proportions of Syrah and Mourvèdre with a minor component of 20% Cabernet Sauvignon. Minor, but essential. "Grange des Pères should have a southern character, but with freshness, and that's what the Cabernet Sauvignon brings," Laurent says.

The Cabernet is planted in the coolest spots, and is always the last variety to harvest. Syrah is planted quite close by, and ripens reliably to make a rich, deep component of the wine. The Mourvèdre is planted a few kilometers away on a hot, south-facing terroir. Tasting barrel samples, you can see what each variety brings to the blend. All are rich and powerful with a good level of tannins, the Syrah full of rich, deep black fruits, the Mourvèdre distinctly

Vineyards at Mas de Daumas Gassac are individual parcels surrounded by woods and trees. Courtesy Mas de Daumas Gassac.

spicy, and the Cabernet herbal and fresh. It's not so much the acidity of the Cabernet as such, but the tightness of its structure that freshens the blend. Without it, the wine would have more of that jammy fruit character of warm climates. So here the Cabernet in effect is playing a moderating role on the forceful fruit character of the other varieties: almost exactly the opposite of the role it plays elsewhere as a "cépage ameliorateur" in strengthening weak varieties. The wines can be quite aromatic when young, but have long aging potential; the 1994 seemed at the midpoint of its development in 2012 and should be good at least for another decade.

Because Cabernet Sauvignon was not permitted under local AOP rules, the first vintages at Mas de Daumas Gassac were labeled as Vin de Table. Subsequently the wines were labeled as IGP Pays d'Hérault, as are those of Grange des Pères, which also is excluded from the AOP because of its content of Cabernet Sauvignon. It's difficult to over-estimate the revolutionary extent of the concept of planting Cabernet Sauvignon at the time, as there was virtually none in the south of France prior to the 1980s. Domaine de Trévallon in

Provence had been the first in 1973, when Eloi Dürrbach produced his 50:50 blend of Cabernet Sauvignon with Syrah.

These three domains produce some of the best known "grand vins" in the south, but they are typical neither of the AOPs nor of the IGPs. Did they lead the way for the subsequent wave of plantings that brought Cabernet Sauvignon and Syrah to prominence in the IGPs of the Languedoc? Not really. Most of the IGP wines originated from an impetus to compete in the market for wines that represent varieties rather than place; this is a completely different level. Varieties and styles were chosen more with an eye on New World competitors than by looking at existing wines and styles. The best wines of the south essentially represent themselves; but as they are sui generis, they have set few precedents and created little in the way of a halo for others in the region.

Roussillon

	cases
AOP Vin Doux Naturel	2,500,000
AOP dry wines	3,500,000
IGP	4,700,000
Vin de France	1,000,000

AOPs (sweet wine)
Banyuls, Maury, Rivesaltes
AOPs (dry wine)
Côtes de Roussillon (& Villages)
Collioure, Maury Sec
IGP
Côtes Catalanes

Moving from Languedoc to Roussillon, the scene changes. Here the region is divided essentially into two large AOPs, Côtes de Roussillon, and Côtes de Roussillon Villages (with several villages now distinguished by the right to add their name to the label). The best known AOPs in the region, Maury, Banyuls, and Rivesaltes, are known for their sweet dessert wines. The climate makes this natural— Roussillon is the hottest and driest Département in France— and the classic sweet wine is the Vin Doux Naturel (VDN), lightly fortified by stopping fermentation by adding distilled spirits (the method is similar to the production of Port but uses less spirits).

The sweet fortified wines of Roussillon are traditionally matured at Mas Amiel for a year in glass bonbons outside, before transfer to foudres for extended aging.

A third of production in Roussillon is devoted to this style, and the region provides the vast majority of fortified wine produced in France.

Until the eighteenth century, sweet wines were made by the technique of passerillage—allowing the berries to stay on the vine long enough to become desiccated. This produces such high sugar levels that there is still residual sugar when fermentation stops, usually around 14% alcohol. The development of distilleries in the eighteenth century allowed passerillage to be replaced by mutage, when fermentation is stopped by adding spirits. Today the production of vin doux naturel in the AOPs is limited to growers of Muscat, Grenache, Macabeo, and Malvoisie. The grapes must have a natural richness with a sugar level of at least 252 g/l (equivalent to 14.5% alcohol), and 5-15% alcohol is added to block fermentation around two thirds of the way through, leaving a sweet wine. However, with the fashion for sweet wines in worldwide decline, the production of VDN has been falling for decades.

Roussillon is still making the painful transition from providing the bulk wines of the Midi towards the higher quality required today. The construction of the railway to Paris in the mid nineteenth century gave a great boost to the region: production increased ten fold in two decades. Phylloxera crushed the region at the end of the century, but after replanting, production was even greater (largely because grafted vines gave double the yields). Total production was around 27 million cases when France entered the European Community, roughly half being Vin de Table. Production today is under half this level, with table wine reduced to about 10%. Even in the past decade, the area of vineyards for table wine has dropped from 40,000 ha to 27,000 ha. A major part of the decline is due to Carignan being pulled out, leaving Grenache as the most important black variety. Relatively new to the area, Syrah is now in second place.

The distinctive features of the wines of Roussillon go back to Roman times, when Muscat was the main grape variety, and wines were made in an oxidized style (today known as rancio). The Muscat appears to have been the finest subvariety, Muscat à Petit Grains; the less refined Muscat of Alexandria (which is also grown as a table grape) was imported later from Spain. In black varieties, Mourvèdre and Grenache have been established since the Middle Ages, with Grenache being used for sweet dessert wines. Roussillon's reputation for dry red wines historically has been that they are the strongest in the south.

A distinction is made between Muscat and other varieties used for sweet wines, as indicated by the use of Muscat in certain appellation names. The Muscat grape is a natural for hot climates, and there are appellations devoted to it scattered all over Languedoc: Muscat de Lunel, Muscat de Mireval, Muscat de Frontignan, and Muscat de Saint Jean de Minervois, all make sweet fortified wines. In Roussillon, where fortified wines are more dominant, Muscat de Rivesaltes is distinguished from Rivesaltes and Maury, where the main varieties are Grenache and Macabeo. The appellation system becomes complicated here, as there are different AOPs for dry wines and sweet wines. In effect, the Rivesaltes AOP for fortified wines more or less overlaps the Côtes de Roussillon and Côtes de Roussillon Villages AOPs for dry wines, and the Banyuls

Reference Wines for Roussillon	
Dry Red	
IGP Côtes Catalanes	*Domaine Gauby* *Olivier Pithon, Le Clot*
Collioure	*Domaine De La Rectorie, La Montagne*
Côtes du Roussillon Villages	*Domaine Gauby, Coume Gineste*
Sweet	
Banyuls	*Domaine de la Rectorie, Cuvée Thérèse Reig*
Maury VDN (modern)	*Mas Amiel, Vintage*
Maury VDN (oxidized)	*Mas Amiel, Classique*
Muscat de Rivesaltes	*Domaine Cazes*

AOP for sweet wines overlaps the Collioure AOP for dry wine. Maury is a rare AOP that now has both dry and sweet wines.

The traditional oxidized styles are made in both vintage and nonvintage (the latter usually coming from a blend of two or three vintages). The key determinant of style is how long the wine ages before it is bottled. In the traditional oxidative style, the wines undergo aging for up to fifteen or twenty years in large wood casks. They can achieve a lovely concentration, but admittedly the oxidized style is an acquired taste. Today it is being partly replaced by wines made in a more modern idiom, using a nonoxidative approach. To avoid confusion, different names are used for the different styles.

Just north of Perpignan, Rivesaltes is divided into three colors: ambré, tuilé, and grenat. The first two are oxidized styles: ambré is essentially white, coming from Grenache, Macabeo, Malvoisie, and

Vineyards of Banyuls extend to the coast.

Muscat, while tuilé is red and excludes Muscat. Hors d'âge indicates ambré or tuilé wines that have had at least five years of élevage under oxidative conditions. Rancio may be added to the label for wines made by traditional oxidative methods. Grenat comes only from Grenache and is made exclusively by reductive methods.

The southernmost AOP in France, Banyuls is the flag carrier for sweet wines. It is divided into three types. The traditional Banyuls is an oxidized style; the Rimage style is a more recent introduction requiring aging for twelve months in an airtight environment. Banyuls Grand Cru is distinguished not by terroir, but by vintage (only the best) and aging (a minimum of 30 months in oak). All types of Grenache (black, gray, and white) are allowed, but Banyuls must have more than 50% Grenache Noir, and Banyuls Grand Cru must have more than 75%.

The same vineyards can be used to make the sweet wines of Banyuls or the dry red wines of Collioure, but there are practical problems in making the transition from sweet to dry wines. The vineyards that are most suitable for achieving very high ripeness to provide berries for making sweet wines may not necessarily be

Inland the vineyards of Banyuls are on steep, convoluted hills.

appropriate for harvesting earlier to make dry wines. "Plots are transitioned to dry wine because they have the right quality—they face north or east—and acquire the appropriate phenolic maturity," explains Jean-Marie Piqué at Mas Amiel.

Banyuls has some of the most striking vineyards in the region. Small vineyards are nestled into the steep hills, and access is difficult. There are amazingly convoluted folds of the hills, with channels for water run-off. The terroir is based on schist, which is evident everywhere. Differences between vineyards are due mostly to exposure and altitude (rising up to 400 m from sea level). "The tendency in reds is towards dry wine in Collioure. Oxidized styles (for Banyuls) are declining," says Jean-Emmanuel Parcé at Domaine de la Rectorie in Banyuls. Another sign of the times is that the focus here is as much on whites and rosé as on reds. An interesting comparison between two cuvées that come from the same Grenache grapes, the dry Collioure l'Oriental and the Banyuls VDN Cuvée Thérèse Reig, shows the first to be an elegant dry wine, very much the style of the south in a modern take; but the Banyuls expresses sweet round black fruits that make you think that perhaps here is the real typicity of Grenache.

It's been possible to make dry as well as sweet wine in Maury since 2011, and the change at Mas Amiel is a sign of the times. Forty years ago, all production was of sweet wines in an oxidized style. Today half of production is dry wine, and a third of that is white (there was no white as recently as ten years ago). The best selling wine in the sweet styles is modern (non oxidized) vintage. This is a sea change in the region.

AOPs for white wine
(Coteaux du) Languedoc
Clairette du Languedoc
Corbières
Faugères
Minervois
Picpoul de Pinet
Saint Chinian
Collioure
Côtes du Roussillon

White wine is very much a minor preoccupation in the Languedoc; overall it is less than 15% of production. It's allowed in only a few of the AOPs. The blended white wines of those AOPs are confined entirely to traditional varieties. In addition, there are two AOPs for varietal wines, Clairette du Languedoc and Picpoul de Pinet. For whites made from traditional southern varieties, but coming from appellations that allow only red wine, Coteaux du Languedoc (now Languedoc) has become the AOP of choice. The break between the AOPs and the IGPs is even more striking for white wine than for red, as the two major white varieties in Languedoc as a whole are Chardonnay and Sauvignon Blanc. Banned from all the AOPs, together they are 40% of all white plantings, and dominate the white IGP wines as varietal labels.

I'm not convinced that either Chardonnay or Sauvignon Blanc makes interesting wines in the south, but another import from the north, Chenin Blanc, makes some of the most interesting whites.

"Chenin Blanc was introduced under the aegis of INAO about twenty years ago to get livelier white wines," explains Vincent Goumard at Mas Cal Demoura. "Because we are in France, there was a tasting after ten years. And the character was rejected as atypical. All the vignerons who took part decided to keep their Chenin, but were forced into the IGP." Vincent's white is IGP Pays d'Hérault, and he adds that, "Of course we have to find calcareous soil to magnify its character. I hope we'll have a white AOP in Larzac; it's a good terroir, and it's a pity but it probably won't happen for another twenty years." A little farther north, Rémy Pédréno at Roc d'Anglade achieves a steely minerality with an IGP de Gard that's a blend of Chenin Blanc with Chardonnay.

The dominant white varieties in the AOPs of the region are Grenache Blanc and Clairette, both somewhat nondescript. There's a tendency to apply more modern techniques to update the style. "Originally the white wines were like all the others of the Languedoc—heavy. Our objective was to have a dry wine with more minerality. It's done with vinification following Burgundy: fermentation in new barriques followed by élevage with battonage," explains Alain Asselin at Domaine du Puech Haut. But is this enough? The problem with the whites of the south, to my mind, is a sort of amorphous aromatic quality, phenolics without flavor, that takes over the palate. One rare example of a white from a quality variety suited to the region is the monovarietal Roussanne from Domaine Les Aurelles. But yields are so low you can see why this might not generally be a viable option. Another example is Prieuré St. Jean de Bébian's white, a blend based on Roussanne, which has moved in recent years from a very ripe to a fresher style.

Indeed, freshness is the key. This makes it all the more remarkable that some of the most interesting whites come from Roussillon. Pushing up against the Spanish border, Roussillon is as hot and dry as it gets in France, but the trend is towards refinement. "In ten years there has been a revolution here. The cooperatives have advanced from the old wines of extraction and alcohol—there are many producers now who make whites based on freshness and balance. Gérard Gauby was the initiator of all this," says Olivier Pithon, whose winery is right in the center of the small town of Calce, a few miles northwest of Perpignan. Gauby's wines are remarkable by any measure.

Reference Wines for White Languedoc-Roussillon		
		Main Variety
IGP Pays d'Hérault	*Mas Cal Demoura, Paroles de Pierres*	*Chenin Blanc*
IGP de Gard	*Roc D'Anglade*	*Chenin Blanc*
IGP Côtes Catalanes	*Domaine Gauby, Coume Gineste*	*Grenache Blanc*
Coteaux du Languedoc	*Domaine les Aurelles, Aurel*	*Roussanne*
	Prieuré St. Jean de Bébian	*Roussanne*

"The profundity of wine does not come from alcohol," Gérard believes. Gauby's wines are notable for their moderate alcohol: around 12.5-13%. Why and how are alcohol levels so much lower here than elsewhere? "I don't use herbicides or pesticides: it's all natural. Phenolic maturity arrives before alcoholic maturity. People say you need 14 or 15 degrees to get Grenache ripe; that's completely mad." Whether or not it's as simple as organic viticulture and early picking, the fact is that the wines, both red and white, are fully ripe yet always retain freshness. The Vieilles Vignes white comes from a blend based on Macabeo and Grenache Blanc, with vines aged from fifty to a hundred years. The top white wine is Coume Gineste, an equal mix of Grenache Blanc and Gris, from terroir based on pure schist. "This is a wine for those who don't understand minerality; after tasting this they will understand minerality," Gérard says. There's also an orange wine (white wine made with red wine methods), La Roque, entirely from Muscat. "This is the oldest variety in the world and we are working it like the Greeks and Romans. We have rediscovered Muscat," Gerard claims. I left Domaine Gauby wondering, as I always do, why other producers can't get the same level of flavor variety and interest without going to extremes. Gauby's reds are as brilliant as his whites, offering a fresh impression of Côtes de Roussillon that few others can match.

Vintages

You might think that vintage variation would be less important in Languedoc-Roussillon as it is the driest and warmest region of France, but even if the summers produce a relatively reliable amount of heat, fluctuations in rainfall from drought to floods, especially at the beginning or end of the season, make for significant variation. However, relatively few wines are made with aging in mind.

2013	*Producers feel the vintage was better than elsewhere in France. After a wet Spring and late start to summer, poor flowering reduced yields; but summer continued into September, and a late harvest gave quality grapes.*
2012	*The vintage can best be described as problematic, with difficulties ranging from drought to mildew during the season, followed by uneven ripening at the end.*
2011	*Rain restored quantities to normal after three drier years, but there are problems with rot in some places.*
2010	*This was a standard year: dry conditions gave good quality, if low quantities.*
2009	*The vintage was as good here as virtually everywhere else in France, with wines achieving high concentration.*
2008	*Drought created problems in the summer, especially difficult for whites, but reds have good concentration.*
2007	*Summer was unusually cool, with more cloud cover than usual, so getting to ripeness was the problem.*
2006	*This is a decent vintage without any special distinguishing*

	characteristic that would make for interesting aging.
2005	This was a good year, and would have rivaled the classic regions elsewhere, but there was some rain at harvest.
2004	This is the most "typical" vintage of the decade, with reliable conditions everywhere in the region and no particular problems.
2003	The year of the heatwave was no easier in Languedoc than anywhere else, and many wines just went over the top.
2002	This was a cloudy summer and the disastrous floods in the Rhône extended into the eastern part of the region.
2001	A hot dry year made for difficult conditions until it rained in September, but this was too late to help those who picked early.
2000	Floods were a problem in November 1999, but after that conditions were good, and the wines are generally good quality.

Vineyard Profiles

Ratings	
***	Excellent producers defining the very best of the appellation
**	Top producers whose wines typify the appellation
*	Very good producers making wines of character that rarely disappoint

Symbols

Address

Phone

Person to contact

Email

Website

Principal AOP

IGP

Red   Rosé   White   Sweet   Reference wines

Grower-producer

Negociant (or purchases grapes)

Cooperative

Lutte raisonnée (sustainable viticulture)

Organic

Biodynamic

Tastings/visits possible

By appointment only

No visits

Sales directly at producer

No direct sales

ha = estate vineyards; bottles = annual production

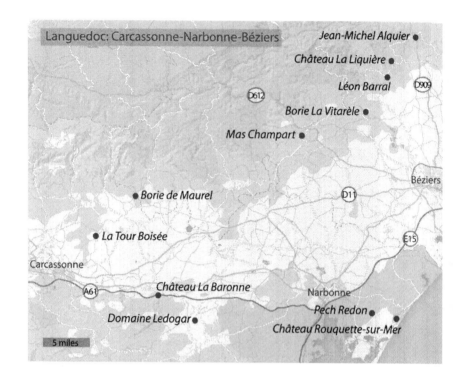

Languedoc: Carcassonne-Narbonne-Béziers

Jean-Michel Alquier ●

Château La Liquière ●

Léon Barral ●

D909

D612

Borie La Vitarèle ●

Mas Champart ●

Béziers

● Borie de Maurel

D11

● La Tour Boisée

E15

Carcassonne

A61

Château La Baronne

Narbonne

Domaine Ledogar ●

Pech Redon ●

Château Rouquette-sur-Mer

5 miles

Languedoc: Beziers-Montpellier-Nîmes

Clos Marie

Roc d'Anglade   Nîmes

Domaine de l'Hortus

Château de la Tuilerie

Montcalmès   Puech Haut

d'Aupilhac
Mas Julien   Grange des Pères

Mas de Daumas Gassac

Mas Cal Delmoura   Alain Chabanon   A750   Montpellier

Les Aurelles   Peyre Rose   A9

Prieuré St. Jean de Bébian

A75

Sète   10 miles

Béziers

Roussillon

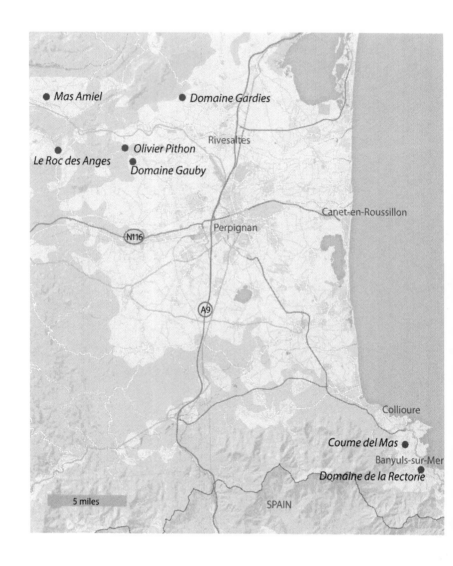

Mas Amiel

Domaine Gardies

Rivesaltes

Olivier Pithon

Le Roc des Anges

Domaine Gauby

Canet-en-Roussillon

N116

Perpignan

A9

Collioure

Coume del Mas

Banyuls-sur-Mer

Domaine de la Rectorie

5 miles

SPAIN

Jean-Michel Alquier **⁣**

4 Route de Pezenes Les Mines, 34600 Faugères

(33) 04 67 23 17 73

@ contact@jmalquier.com

Jean-Michel Alquier

Faugères

Faugères, La Maison Jaune

12 ha; 50,000 bottles

The winery is located in the center of town, with the cellar just opposite the family house. "I am the fifth generation on the property," says Jean-Michel. His grandfather left the area to become a negociant in Paris, but his father, Gilbert, returned, and began to renew the vineyards in the 1960s, with a focus on Syrah. "This was how the domain began to acquire its present reputation," Jean-Michel explains. The domain was split after Gilbert's death between Jean-Michel and Frédéric Alquier, and it's Jean-Michel's wines that are now considered to be a leading light of the appellation. There's only one hectare for white grapes. For red wines, vineyards are divided according to position on the slope (all south-facing) to make three cuvées: La Première (half Syrah) comes from the base of the slope where the soils are deepest; Maison Jaune comes from the slope and is more structured, although it's 70% Grenache; and Les Bastides comes from the top of the hill and is always very ripe, although it's 70% old vines Syrah. All the wines are matured in barrique. The style here is modern, but the wines display it in different ways. La Première has a freshness you would not have seen in Faugères ten or twenty years ago, satisfying the objective of being ready to drink soonest. Maison Jaune has a smoothness and elegance that shows the progress of recent years. And Les Bastides has structure rather than simple expression of overt fruit, requiring at least a decade to begin to open up.

Roc d'Anglade

700 Chemin de Vignecroze, 30980 Langlade

04 66 81 45 83

contact@rocdanglade.fr

Rémy Pédréno

www.rocdanglade.fr

IGP de Gard

IGP de Gard

IGP de Gard

10 ha; 35,000 bottles

Winemaking is a second career for Rémy Pédréno. He had been a computer programmer for nine years when he discovered wine, and started by making a single barrique in his parents' garage. He became the winemaker when René Rostaing (from Côte Rôtie) wanted to make wine in the south in 1998, and then in 2002 he bought his own vines and became independent. The winery has two storeys, located under the family residence. Vineyards are in various parcels in the vicinity. Rémy is an enthusiast for Carignan, to the point that his wines are labeled as IGP de Gard because he wants to include more Carignan than is permitted in the AOP. He makes his point with the concentration and elegance of an experimental Vieilles Vignes cuvée of Carignan from 2007. In the regular cuvée, the red is around half Carignan, with Grenache, Syrah and (in recent vintages) Mourvèdre. It's a wine that's very expressive of vintage, from a positively Burgundian 2002, to a savory 2004 with mineral overtones, and then a more typically southern 2011, but all vintages show a sense of reserve and elegance. "If you asked me to produce a wine to show why I chose this métier, this is the wine I would show today," Rémy says about his 2002 vintage. The rosé is based on Mourvèdre, and the white on Chenin Blanc, a good example of breaking out of the southern straightjacket by moving to more northern varieties. The white has lots of character, developing in a savory, mineral direction.

Domaine d'Aupilhac

28 rue du Plo, 34150 Montpeyroux

(33) 04 67 96 61 19

aupilhac@wanadoo.fr

Sylvain Fadat

www.aupilhac.com

Languedoc-Montpeyroux

Languedoc, Les Cocalières

25 ha; 130,000 bottles

Sylvain Fadat is the fifth generation of vignerons in the family, but was the first to bottle his own wine in 1989. At that time the domain was still involved in polyculture, but since 1992 it has been concerned exclusively with viticulture. Its headquarters are in an unassuming house along what used to be the route for the stagecoach through Montpeyroux. But behind the house is a winery full of modern equipment. The main vineyards are at Aupilhac (close to Montpeyroux), including some extending directly behind the property, but there is another vineyard at Cocalières with an elevation of 350 m, where Sylvain planted vines on a steeply terraced hillside in 1998. The focus is on traditional Southern varieties: Carignan, Grenache, Cinsault, Mourvèdre, and Syrah for the reds, with Roussanne, Marsanne, Grenache Blanc, and Vermentino for the whites. It was the reds that established the reputation of the Domaine, all made by traditional methods of vinification. The wines are mostly labeled as Languedoc (formerly Coteaux du Languedoc), with the best cuvées in the category of Languedoc-Montpeyroux. Sylvain is known as somewhat of a specialist in Carignan, and Le Carignan, a monovarietal cuvée from 60-year-old vines, is one of the domain's best-known wines. (It's an IGP Mont Baudile, as is the monovarietal Cinsault.) It's a sign of progress in the area that Sylvain was a trendsetter in 1990 but is now one of several good producers in Montpeyroux.

Domaine Les Aurelles

SOLEN

2001

COTEAUX
DU
LANGUEDOC

DOMAINE LES AURELLES
14,5% Vol. PRODUIT DE FRANCE 750 ml
MIS EN BOUTEILLE AU DOMAINE
GAEC LES AURELLES 34320 NIZAS

8 chemin des Champs Blancs, 34320 Nizas

(33) 04 67 98 46 21

contact@les-aurelles.com

Basile Saint Germain

www.les-aurelles.com

Languedoc-Pézenas

Languedoc-Pézenas, Aurel

9 ha; 25,000 bottles

Wine is in the family background as Caroline Saint Germain comes from Cognac, but the creation of Les Aurelles in 1995 was a new career for Basil Saint Germain. He was influenced by two years spent at Château Latour. "I chose this particular area because the first wine of the Languedoc I tasted came from here, and because the terroir seemed to resemble Château Latour, with an area of gravel," he says. Vineyards are located where alluvial deposits created a deep layer of gravel; plantings are Carignan, Mourvèdre, Syrah, and Grenache, with some Roussanne for white wine. The winery is a modern concrete bunker constructed on a high point in Nizas in 2001. The domain is committed to organic viticulture to the point of including a statement on the back label certifying the absence of pesticides. Yields are low, under 25 hl/ha for reds and under 18 hl/ha for white. Basil is a devotée of Carignan, and has planted new vines as well as buying all the old vines he can find. There are three cuvées of red and one white. After the entry level Déelle (a blend that changes with vintage), come Solen (Grenache, Carignan, and Syrah) and Aurel (Mourvèdre, Syrah, and Grenache). These express vintage: Solen shows its best qualities in cooler years, while Aurel really requires warmer years for the Mourvèdre's character to emerge. The white Aurel is Roussanne. The style is moderate, in line with Basil's purpose: "I want above all to make a wine to have with food not to win competitions."

Château La Baronne

LA BARONNE

NOTRE DAME
2005
FAMILLE LIGNÈRES - FONTCOUVERTE
LANGUEDOC-ROUSSILLON

 21 rue Jean Jaurès, Moux 11700

 (33) 04 68 43 90 20

 info@chateaulabaronne.com

 Paul Lignères

 www.chateaulabaronne.com

 Corbières

Corbières, Alaric

90 ha; 250,000 bottles

The Lignères have the unusual characteristic of being medically qualified, although their main interest is now wine. The domain was founded by André and Suzette in 1957, and is now run by their three children. Visits start at the headquarters in Moux, where wines for all their three domains are bottled. Château La Baronne is the most important; nearby are Las Vals and Plo de Maorou. Vineyards lie between Moux and Fontcouverte under the lee of calcareous mountains, with elevations around 100-200 m making for late harvests. Black varieties are 90% of plantings. The winery has a mix of all sorts of cuves: concrete, stainless steel, and wood. There are also experiments with amphorae (made by a local potter from clay from the same terroir as the wines). Vineyards are in Corbières, but several monovarietal cuvées are bottled as IGP Hauterive, including Notre Dame (Syrah), and Les Vals (Mourvèdre for red and Roussanne for white). The most interesting of the monovarietals is Pièce de Roche, from a 4 ha plot of Carignan planted in 1892. Carignan is a focus of the domain, occupying more than a third of the vineyard area. It figures in the blends under the Corbières AOP: Les Lanes (Grenache and Carignan), Les Chemins (Grenache, Syrah and Carignan), and Alaric (Syrah, Carignan, and Mourvèdre). There's a focus on low sulfur, and Les Chemins de Traverse is a cuvée bottled without added sulfur. "We are looking for light extraction," is how Paul Lignères describes the style.

Domaine Léon Barral

Hameau de Lenthéric, Cabrerolles, 34480

(33) 04 67 90 29 13

Léon Barral

www.domaineleonbarral.com

Faugères

Faugères

33 ha; 90,000 bottles

This committed biodynamic domain is well known for its natural wines, and when I arrived, Didier Barral was about to set out to move his cows to new pasture. He has a herd of around 40 cows, not to mention some horses and pigs; during summer they graze on pastures near the vineyards, then during winter they are allowed into the vines. "We do polyculture, to get balance you have to have polyculture," explains Didier, under the enquiring gaze of the cows, some of which are a recreated medieval breed. Didier founded the domain in 1993 (it is named after his grandfather). It consists of many vineyard parcels, varying from 0.3 to 5 ha in size, with many old vines. The vineyards look quite old fashioned, with the vines pruned in gobelet style as free-standing bushes. "This makes a parasol for the sun, which is important. I don't think a trellis is well adapted to the climate," Didier maintains. Back in the cave, a stone building in the hamlet of Lenthéric, a tasting of barrel samples runs through many varieties, each still separate in barrique. Each variety shows its character through the prism of a highly refined style—even Carignan. The single white cuvée is based on the old variety of Terret Blanc and is an IGP Pays d'Hérault. The three reds cuvées are Faugères, the Faugères Jadis, and the Faugères Valinière, the first two being half Grenache, but the last more than three quarters Mourvèdre. Fine, tight, and precise would be a fair description of house style.

Domaine Borie de Maurel

rue de La Sallèle, 34210 Félines-Minervois

(33) 04 68 91 68 58

contact@boriedemaurel.fr

Michel Escande

www.boriedemaurel.fr

Minervois

35 ha; 200,000 bottles

A young domain, Borie de Maurel was founded in 1989 by Sylvie et Michel Escande (who abandoned a nautical career) as part of the return to the land movement in the Languedoc. The domain is located in the heart of Minervois, by La Livinière, one of the Crus of the Languedoc. The Escandes started by buying 5 ha of vineyards and a rather dilapidated house. Steady expansion has made this one of the larger domains in the area, and the next generation, Gabriel and Maxime, are now involved. Vineyards are on steep slopes, and significant heterogeneity in the terroirs (roughly divided between warmer sandstone and cooler limestone) is matched by the diversity of grape varieties, many vinified as monovarietals. All the wines are under the Minervois label, coming from different varieties or blends: Rève de Carignan and Sylla (100% Syrah) use carbonic maceration for softening the flavor profile, while Maxime (100% Mourvèdre) and Belle de Nuit (100% Grenache) are vinified conventionally. The Sylla cuvée was the wine that made the reputation of the domain in the early nineties. The introductory wine, Esprit d'Automne, is a blend of Syrah, Carignan, and Grenache, while the Minervois La Livinière, La Feline, is a blend of two thirds Syrah with one third Grenache and a little Carignan; it's matured a third in barriques and two thirds in cuve. Most production is red, but there is a white, La Belle Aude, which is 90% Marsanne and 10% Muscat.

Borie La Vitarèle

 34430 Causses-et-Veyran

📞 (33) 04 67 89 50 43

@ jf.izarn@borielavitarele.fr

Cathy Izarn

🌐 www.borielavitarele.fr

St. Chinian

🍾 St. Chinian, Les Schistes

19 ha; 60,000 bottles

Cathy and Jean-François Izarn bought this 100 ha estate, located up a dirt track a few miles from the village of Causses-et-Veyran in 1986. It was mostly virgin land, and has been gradually built up to its present size, with vineyards in several separate parcels. Plantings are 40% Syrah and 40% Grenache, with smaller amounts of Merlot, Mourvèdre, Carignan, and white varieties. "We look for concentration but we don't want anything massive. We want refinement more than power," is how Jean-François explained his objectives. "We use very little new oak, we want to respect the terroir. I like to represent the unique character, the particularité of each terroir. It's more interesting to make cuvées from each terroir in a Burgundian way rather than to follow the Bordeaux model and make a grand vin and second wine." In reds, there is an introductory cuvée (Les Cigales: "This is my equivalent to rosé, I don't like rosé but this is easy to drink"), three cuvées from specific terroirs (Terres Blanches from calcareous soils, Les Schistes from schist on the slopes, and Les Crès from galets): these become progressively richer. Midi Rouge is the grand wine of the domain, made in small amounts from a blend of varieties and terroirs. The style is rich, in the direction of the generosity of Châteauneuf-du-Pape, something of a modern take on the tradition of the Languedoc. Sadly, Jean-François died in an accident in April 2014, but Cathy continues to run the domain.

Mas Cal Demoura

 Route de Saint André, 34725 Jonquières

📞 (33) 04 67 88 61 51

@ info@caldemoura.com

Vincent Goumard

🌐 www.caldemoura.com

Terrasses du Larzac

🍷 L'Infidèle

IGP Pays d'Hérault, Parole de Pierres

14 ha; 45,000 bottles

Isabelle and Vincent Goumard took over Mas Cal Demoura in 2004 on the retirement of Jean-Pierre Jullien, who had created the estate in 1993. Vincent was a consultant in Paris before he took up wine as a second career. The winery is a small practical facility packed with equipment. Vineyards are in two main groups on either side of Jonquières. The majority have clay-calcareous soils, and are planted with black grapevines, including all five varieties of the appellation; the rest have calcareous pebbles and are where the white varieties are planted, mostly Chenin Blanc (going back to an experiment of the 1990s), with smaller quantities of the usual southern varieties. Wines are matured in a mixture of demi-muids and barriques (except for the more aromatic white varieties, which are vinified in cuve). There are three red cuvées, two whites, and a rosé. L'Infidèle is the principal red cuvée, a blend of all five varieties. Coming from a selection of pebbly parcels, Les Combariolles is mainly Syrah and Mourvèdre, and is the most structured wine of the house. At the other extreme is Feu Sacré, based on old vines Grenache. In the whites, L'Etincelle is half Chenin Blanc, but the top white wine, Paroles de Pierres, is three quarters Chenin with Roussanne making up most of the rest of the blend. The style varies quite a bit through the reds, but tends to be smooth and harmonious. The whites have a fresh character far removed from the old amorphous phenolics of the south.

Domaine Alain Chabanon

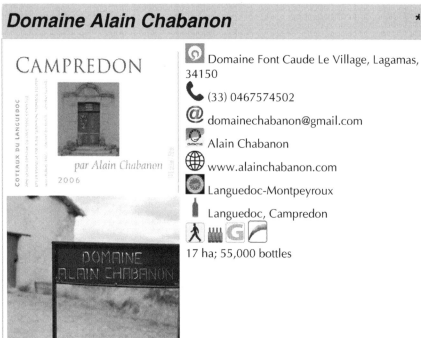

CAMPREDON

par Alain Chabanon
2006

COTEAUX DU LANGUEDOC

Domaine Font Caude Le Village, Lagamas, 34150

(33) 0467574502

domainechabanon@gmail.com

Alain Chabanon

www.alainchabanon.com

Languedoc-Montpeyroux

Languedoc, Campredon

17 ha; 55,000 bottles

After qualifying in oenology at Bordeaux and Montpellier, and serving an apprenticeship with Alain Brumont in Madiran, Alain Chabanon returned to his roots in the Languedoc where he purchased vineyards between Jonquières and Montpeyroux. His first vintage was 1992 (only 2,500 bottles). A new winery was built in 2001. Originally the domain was called Font Caude (named for a nearby warm spring), but now the wines are labeled as Domaine Chabanon. Alain produces a wide range of wines, including Languedoc, IGP d'Oc, and Vin de France, from vineyards spread over several communes just below the Terrasses de Larzac. Under IGP and Vin de France are wines from varieties that aren't common in the region, including Chenin Blanc and Vermentino (Trélans is a blend of two thirds Vermentino to one third Chenin Blanc), and Merlot (this is the well-regarded Merle aux Alouettes cuvée); the Languedoc AOP wines are GSM (Grenache-Syrah-Mourvèdre) or Syrah plus Mourvèdre. In fact, the first wine of the domain was the l'Esprit de Font Caude blend of equal proportions of Syrah and Mourvèdre. There are nine cuvées altogether, the idea being to demonstrate the characters of the very different plots. "This is not a range from petit vin to a grand vin, it's several different choices to suit different tastes, sometimes at the same price so that consumers aren't tempted to choose by cost. Of course, some are ready to drink today and others need three years," Alain explains.

Mas Champart

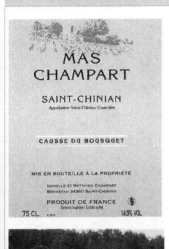

34360 Saint Chinian

(33) 04 67 38 20 09

mas-champart@wanadoo.fr

Matthieu Champart

St. Chinian

St. Chinian, Causse du Bousquet

16 ha; 40,000 bottles

Isabelle and Mathieu Champart moved from Paris to take over an old farm in 1976; with no experience in winemaking, grapes were sold to the cooperative until 1988 when they began to bottle their own wine. A winery was constructed in 1995. Since taking over, they have expanded the estate from its original 8 ha, sometimes by buying abandoned vineyards of old vines. In addition to the vineyards, the property includes another 8 ha of other fruits and crops. The vineyards comprise around twenty small plots on limestone hills, at altitudes between 200 m and 300 m. Grenache is grown on the higher locations, Syrah on north-facing slopes, and Mourvèdre on the clay-limestone terraces. The wines come in all three colors of St. Chinian, with three different red cuvées: going up the scale, Côte d'Arbo is a classic blend aged in vat (a lively introductory wine); Causse de Bousquet is two thirds Syrah with Mourvèdre and Grenache, aged partly in vat and partly in barrel (this is the major wine of the domain); and Clos de la Simonette is almost three quarters Mourvèdre (the rest is Grenache) aged in demi muids. The white St. Chinian is a conventional blend of local varieties. The Champarts' interests include some grapes that aren't allowed in the St. Chinian AOP, so there's an unusual IGP d'Oc which is a blend of 70% Cabernet Franc to 30% Syrah, and a white IGP Pays d'Hérault made from 80% Terret and 20% Grenache Gris.

Coume del Mas

COUME DEL MAS 2008

COLLIOURE
APPELLATION COLLIOURE CONTRÔLÉE
MIS EN BOUTEILLE AU DOMAINE · VIGNOBLE DE LA COUME DEL MAS
66650 BANYULS SUR MER · FRANCE · PRODUCT OF FRANCE
750 ML

3 Rue Alphonse Daudet, 66650 Banuyls-sur-Mer

(33) 04 68 88 37 03

philippegard@libertysurf.fr

Philippe Gard

www.coumedelmas.com

Banyuls

15 ha; 40,000 bottles

This domain was created by Philippe and Nathalie Gard in 2001 (after Philippe consulted for several domains in Chablis and Pomerol), when they purchased vineyards mostly around the lieu-dit of Coume del Mas, but with outlying plots scattered all over the hills surrounding Banyuls-sur-Mer. The domain expanded from its original 2 ha to its present thirty parcels. The focus was to find old vines, and the majority of plantings are old bush vines of Grenache. The domain produces both the VDN (sweet) Banyuls and also the dry style of Banyuls Blanc, dry red under the Collioure AOP, and a rosé. Altogether there are about eight cuvées; sweet wines are about 20% of production. The flagship wine is Quadratur, a blend of Grenache, Carignan and Mourvèdre that spends 12 months in oak. By contrast, Schistes is a monovarietal old vines Grenache that is fermented and matured exclusively in stainless steel. Given the amount of manual (or equine) labor required to maintain the vines, the Coume del Mas domain has now reached its size limit, but has become quite a wide-ranging enterprise as another set of wines comes from Mas Christine, a separate property leased nearby in the Côtes de Roussillon appellation. In addition. Philippe runs a negociant business, Tramontane Wines, in association with winemaker Andy Cook, who is also a partner in Mas Christine. The Consolation range comes from selections from Coume del Mas, Mas Christine and other sources.

Mas de Daumas Gassac ★★

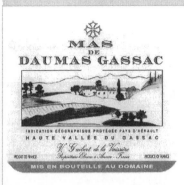

 Mas Daumas, 34150 Aniane

☎ (33) 04 67 57 71 28

@ contact@daumas-gassac.com

Samuel Guibert

⊕ www.daumas-gassac.com

◉ IGP Pays d'Hérault

🍶 IGP Pays d'Hérault

🚶♨🅶🅽🍷

40 ha; 205,000 bottles

Aimé Guibert was looking for a country house when he purchased the estate in 1970. The geographer Henri Enjalbert, a family friend, suggested that the Gassac valley, with red glacial soils and a microclimate of cool nights, was suitable for wine production. Emile Peynaud from Bordeaux became a consultant, and the creation of the domain pioneered the production of high quality wine in Languedoc. Today the domain has about 50 small individual vineyards separated by the original garrigue. Based on Cabernet Sauvignon, but with many subsidiary varieties, the red wine is by no means a typical Cabernet. "We are not looking for the modern jammy fruity style. We belong more to the Bordeaux 1961 attitude—wine with 12.5% alcohol and good acidity," says Samuel Guibert. Older vintages seem to alternate between Atlantic austerity and the spices and herbs of the Mediterranean garrigue, with long aging potential: the 1982 and 1983 vintages were still vibrant in 2013. Current vintages are more forward but less complex. The white is based on a blend of Chardonnay, Viognier, and Petit Manseng, with the balance from many other varieties. In addition to the regular cuvées, there is now a cuvée Emile Peynaud in some vintages; made from the oldest Cabernet Sauvignon vines in one of the original vineyards, it is powerful in the modern idiom. Moulin de Gassac is a negociant line that includes purchased grapes. Success is indicated by the constant stream of visitors to the tasting room.

Domaine Gardiés

Chemin de Montpins, 66600 Espira d'Agly

(33) 04 68 64 61 16

domgardies@wanadoo.fr

Jean Gardiés

www.domaine-gardies.fr

Côtes du Roussillon Villages

40 ha; 100,000 bottles

Jean Gardiés took over the family domaine in 1990. Previously the wine had been sold off in bulk, but he started bottling in 1993. A new wooden winery was built at Espira de l'Agly in 2006. Vineyards are located in two somewhat different terroirs, on the chalky-clay soils of Vingrau (where the family originated), and the black schist of Espira de l'Agly north of Perpignan. The older vines are at Vingrau, with newer plantings at Espira de l'Agly. The major plantings are black varieties, on the south- and east-facing slopes, with some white varieties on north-facing slopes in Vingrau at higher altitudes to retain freshness. Black varieties are Grenache and Carignan; whites are Grenache Blanc and Roussanne. There are four series of wines. The introductory wines, red, rosé, and white, are Côtes du Roussillon, blended from various holdings, while both red and white Le Clos des Vignes come specifically from Vingrau (the red is a Côtes du Roussillon Tautavel). The top of the line reds come from lower yields; La Torre is based on a blend dominated by Mourvèdre from Espira de l'Agly; and Les Falaises is dominated by Carignan from Vingrau. Although production has decreased, there is also a series of sweet wines from Rivesaltes, including a Muscat de Rivesaltes: "These sweet wines are a difficult sell outside of France, which is a pity as it's a unique tradition to the Roussillon," Jean says. Most of the wine is sold to restaurants in France.

Domaine Gauby ★★★

DOMAINE
GAUBY
2010

Coume Gineste

Côtes du Roussillon Villages

Appellation Côtes du Roussillon Villages Contrôlée

MIS EN BOUTEILLE AU DOMAINE
DOMAINE GAUBY 66600 CALCE
PRODUCE OF FRANCE

ALC. 14 % BY VOL. 1500ML

 66600 Calce

📞 (33) 04 68 64 35 19

@ domaine.gauby@wanadoo.fr

 Gerard Gauby

🌐 www.domainegauby.fr

 Côtes du Roussillon Villages

🍾 Muntada

🍾 Coume Gineste

43 ha; 90,000 bottles

The entrance to Domaine Gauby is an intimidating one-car-wide track along the ridge above a valley just outside Calce, 30-40 km northwest of Perpignan, at an elevation around 350-450 m. Half of the valley is given over to vineyards, the other half remaining in its natural state to maintain the ecosystem: "We practice polyculture, I don't believe in monoculture. We've planted cereals, olive trees, and almond trees," says Gérard Gauby. In 2003, winemaking moved from a garage in the town of Calce to a purpose built chai under the family house in the middle of the valley. Soils are based on deep, friable schist at the bottom of the valley with calcareous components higher up. Plantings are two thirds red. The whites are IGP Côtes de Catalanes and the reds are AOP Côtes du Roussillon Villages. Tasting here is an exercise in understanding extreme precision and elegance, reinforced by moderate alcohol, rarely above 12.5% yet always fully ripe. When tasting, Gérard instructs you not to swirl the wine but to let the complexity of the aromas "montent tranquillement." The whites are remarkable for their freshness. The reds extend from the classic blend of Vieilles Vignes, to the Grenache-based La Roque from old vines. Coume Gineste comes from friable schist, and Muntada comes from the same terroir as La Roque but is based on Syrah. The deepest red is La Founa, based on a complex mix of prephylloxera vines. Almost nothing here is less than exceptional for the region.

Domaine de La Grange des Pères   ★★★

34150 Aniane

☎ (33) 04 67 57 70 55

Laurent Vaillé

IGP Pays d'Hérault

15 ha; 30,000 bottles

Laurent Vaillé established his domain in 1989 on ungiving terroir of hard limestone by dynamiting and bulldozing to clear land for planting. The winery is actually in the middle of uncultivated fields with not a vine in sight, but the Syrah and Cabernet vineyards are fairly close by, the main difference being that Cabernet is planted in the cooler exposures. Mourvèdre is 4-5 km away, on a rather hot south-facing plot covered in galets. The red wine for which the domain is famous is a blend of 40% Syrah, 40% Mourvèdre, and 20% Cabernet Sauvignon. "The Cabernet Sauvignon is like salt in food. I do not want Cabernet Sauvignon to dominate my assemblage," says Laurent. Vines are grown low to the ground. Yields are always very low, often below 25 hl/ha. There are only two wines here, one red and one white. Laurent is a perfectionist: "Any lot that isn't satisfactory is discarded, I don't want to make a second wine." Laurent refuses to draw any distinction between vins de garde and wines to drink now, but in my view the red wine needs considerable age to show its best. The 1994 showed a seamless elegance in 2012, with a subtlety comparable to a top northern Rhône. The 2000 vintage was still dense and rich at this point; and it was vinicide to drink the 2008 or 2009, because sheer power and aromatics hid much of their potential. Only 10% of production, a white wine is based on Roussanne with smaller amounts of Marsanne and Chardonnay.

Domaine de L'Hortus

2007
CLASSIQUE

l'H bergerie ORTUS

PIC SAINT LOUP

COTEAUX DU LANGUEDOC
APPELLATION COTEAUX DU LANGUEDOC CONTROLEE

MIS EN BOUTEILLE À FRANCE
34270 PAR JEAN ORLIAC, DOMAINE DE L'HORTUS
34270 VALFLAUNES - PRODUIT DE FRANCE
17312

Valflaunès, 34270

(33) 04 67 55 31 20

contact@domaine-hortus.fr

Famille Orliac

www.domaine-hortus.fr

Pic St. Loup

Pic St. Loup, Grand Cuvée

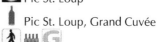

77 ha; 350,000 bottles

The winery occupies a new, purpose-built building surrounded by carefully tended vines. The domain is in the center of Pic St. Loup, where its first vines were planted right under the cliffs of Mount Hortus. There was nothing here in 1979 when Jean and Marie-Thérèse Orliac started to construct the estate, which has been built up, little by little with many separate parcels. Now their sons Yves and Martin are involved. This is a very lively enterprise: the family gathers for lunch each day at the winery, and conversation to say the least is spirited. There are three red cuvées, two whites, and a rosé. The entry-level wines are labeled as Bergerie de l'Hortus, and are intended for relatively rapid consumption. The Grande Cuvée label of Domaine de l'Hortus indicates wines that are intended to be more vin de garde. The Clos du Prieur red comes from the most recent acquisition, ten years ago, of a vineyard in Terraces de Larzac, about 20 miles to the west (where the climate is distinctly more Continental). " The vineyards have reached their size: there are no new plantings planned. It's the story of the 2000s; we replanted some abandoned vineyards, but now we have finished, " says Jean Orliac. The style is modern. " We look for wines that aren't too powerful but have some finesse, " says Martin Orliac. The Bergerie wines are very approachable, but I find the Grand Cuvée more mainstream, while the restraint of Clos du Prieur is attractive and ageworthy.

Domaine Ledogar

◉ Place de la République, 11200 Ferrals les Corbières

📞 04 68 32 67 85

@ contact@domaineledogar.fr

👤 Xavier Ledogar

🌐 www.domaineledogar.fr

◼ Corbières

🍾 Vin de France, La Mariole

19 ha; 40,000 bottles

Four generations of Ledogars have been making wine in Corbières, but it was only when Xavier Ledogar decided he wanted to become a vigneron that his father, André, decided to create his own domain (initially called Domaine Grand Lauze, renamed Domaine Ledogar in 2008). They purchased an old building in 1997, and made the first vintage in 1998. Xavier's younger brother Mathieu joined the domain in 2000. The domain is committed to producing natural wine, and as a result has run into the usual difficulties with the *agrément* for the AOP; so although 80% of their vineyards are in Corbières and 20% in IGP, some of the wines are labeled as Vin de France. Within Corbières, plantings are mostly Carignan (11 ha), Mourvèdre (2.5 ha), Syrah (2.5 ha), or Grenache (2 ha); the rest consists of Maccabeu and Cinsault, and a small amount of white varieties. Yields are low, at 25-35 hl/ha. In addition there are some IGP vineyards that André had planted with Cabernet Sauvignon and Marselan. There are some plots in Corbières of very old Carignan and Grenache, within which are some other old varieties of the area. The top wines of the domain come from Carignan or Carignan-dominated blends. Rather spicy, the Corbières is a conventional blend, but Tout Natur, a Vin de France blend of Carignan with Mourvèdre, would make a fine Corbières if it had the agrément. Coming from very old vines, La Mariole is a monovarietal Carignan with a rare precision.

Château de La Liquière

La Liquière, 34480 Cabrerolles

(33) 04 67 90 29 20

info@chateaulaliquiere.com

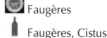 François Vidal

www.chateaulaliquiere.com

Faugères

Faugères, Cistus

65 ha; 280,000 bottles

The modern tasting room is located in an old castle in the center of the town of Cabrerolles. The vineyards are in many different parcels scattered throughout all four villages of Faugères. "The domain has increased since the 1960s but now we have decided not to grow any more," says François Villard, whose grandparents established the domain in the 1960s. Vinification by parcel produces 50 different lots, and it's only later that the decision is made on which to bottle as separate cuvées and which to blend together. There are five red cuvées, three whites, and two rosés. The entry level line goes under the name of Les Amandiers and is matured in concrete and steel. The white Cistus has a few months maturation in new oak barriques, new because the period is short; and then the barriques are used to mature the red wine. Amandiers comes from wines at lower altitudes, and Cistus from those higher up, so there's a correlation at Liquière between the top of the hill and the top of the scale. A Vieilles Vignes red cuvée comes from a blend of old vines of Carignan and Grenache; and the Nos Racines cuvée comes from a 110-year-old plot of Carignan that's planted in a field blend with some other old varieties. It's a paradox that these are the oldest vines but the wine seems the most modern in the range. The house style is round and smooth and elegant (although of course there is some stylistic variation from the entry level to the top wines).

Clos Marie

Route de Cazeneuve, 34270 Lauret

(33) 04 67 59 06 96

clos.marie@orange.fr

Christophe Peyrus

Pic St. Loup

Pic St. Loup, Metairies du Clos

23 ha; 95,000 bottles

The winery is a tiny property in the center of the little town of Lauret where Françoise Julien and Christophe Peyrus make the wine. The estate was worked by Christophe's grandfather (who made wine) and father (who sent grapes to the coop), but Françoise and Christophe created Clos Marie as a domain when they decided to produce wine in 1992. They began with 8 ha, and today there are various parcels scattered around Lauret in the Pic St. Loup AOP. There are four red cuvées, two whites, and one rosé. Terroir is the main criterion for distinguishing the cuvées—even in Pic St. Loup there are variations of terroir, says Françoise—but there are also differences in assemblage and age of vines (with one cuvée coming from young vines). The objective is for Clos Marie to be mineral with freshness and precision. "It's very important to keep alcohol low to maintain freshness; we do vendange vert and pick relatively early," explains Françoise. Viticulture is organic with some biodynamic treatments. Each parcel is vinified separately. "Originally each variety was vinified separately, but then we found we got better results with cofermentation." Wines are matured in oak, but there is no new wood. The style here is a long way from the old stereotype of the region: both reds and whites are light and fresh, in particular the red Metairies du Clos, which comes from old vines. Alcohol levels are moderate for the region. This is a standard bearer for the new style of the Languedoc.

Domaine du Mas Amiel

PRODUCT OF FRANCE

MAS AMIEL

LE PLAISIR

2004

CÔTES DU ROUSSILLON

NET CONT. 750 ML   ROSE TABLE WINE   ALC. 13.5% BY VOL.

 Maury, 66460

 (33) 04 68 29 01 02

 contact@masamiel.fr

 www.masamiel.fr

 Maury

Maury, Vintage

170 ha; 350,000 bottles

The history of this large domain, located just outside Maury, is somewhat chequered; won in a game of cards from the Bishop of Perpignan in 1816, it became the property of a bank when the owners were ruined in 1909, and then in 1999 was sold to Olivier Decelle (former owner of a frozen food retailer), who has set about renovating the vineyards (several hectares are replanted each year) and chais. Its fame was established for sweet fortified wines, but in the past couple of decades it has been making a transition to a point at which half the wines are dry. The old cellar is used for maturing traditional wines, but there is now a new cellar with temperature-controlled cuves for the new lines of dry wines. The vineyards are on slopes surrounding the winery, generally on soils of schist. There are dry whites and reds under the AOP Côtes de Roussillon; and recently four cuvées of dry red wines from old vines and single vineyards have been introduced under the new Maury Sec label. The sweet wines divide into the modern Vintage line and the traditionally oxidative Classique line. Oxidative wines start out with a year in glass demi-johns in the sun, and then mature in large foudres. Vintage-dated VDNs are produced about once every decade; other Classique wines come from a blend of two or three vintages, and are labeled by their average age as 15-year or 20-year. Although no longer in fashion, the sweet wines remain a benchmark; the dry wines have yet to catch up.

Mas Jullien **⋆⋆

MIS EN BOUTEILLE AU MAS

Route Saint André, Jonquières, 34725

(33) 04 67 96 60 04

masjullien@free.fr

Olivier Jullien

Terrasses du Larzac

Languedoc, Mas Jullien

20 ha; 70,000 bottles

Mas Jullien was started by Olivier Jullien in 1985 (the same year the AOC of Coteaux du Languedoc was created), when he was twenty. (His father, Jean-Pierre, was a grower who sent his grapes to the coop. He started Mas Cal Demoura next door after Olivier's success, and later sold it.) The winery has grown into a collection of buildings, with a tasting room to accommodate the constant trek of visitors. From a small start with 3 ha of rented vines, the domain has expanded into many separate holdings with various soil types, with many changes in the vineyard holdings over the years. Olivier is still buying and selling vineyards to balance the terroirs: there is a sense of restless movement here, with Olivier often giving the impression he wants to be off to the next thing. Based on the traditional Southern varieties of Carignan, Grenache, Cinsault, Syrah, and Mourvèdre, there are three red cuvées (all Terrasses de Larzac AOP). The principal cuvée is called simply Mas Jullien. The introductory wine is Les Derniers Etats de l'Ame (a reference to an earlier cuvée, L'Etat de l'Ame, which Olivier had proposed to stop producing, but resumed after protests). Its constitution changes from year to year. The top wine, Carlan, is a parcel selection from terroir of schist (in some years there are also other parcel selections). The single white cuvée, a blend of Carignan Blanc and Chenin Blanc, is IGP Pays d'Hérault. There are also a rosé (with the varieties changing each year), and a dessert wine, Cartagène.

Domaine de Montcalmès

Chemin du Cimetière, 34150 Puéchabon

04.67.57.74.16

gaecbh@wanadoo.fr

Frédéric Pourtalié

www.domainedemontcalmes.fr

Terrasses du Larzac

Terrasses du Larzac

23 ha; 60,000 bottles

His grandfather produced wine, but his father sold grapes to the coop, until Frédéric Pourtalié took over the domain in 1998, after working elsewhere in the south, with internships at Grange des Pères and Alain Graillot. His first vintage was in 1999, just 5,000 bottles for the domain. The entrance to the winery is quite unassuming, just an ordinary building off the main street in Puéchabon, but behind are extensive caves packed with stainless steel tanks for fermentation and barriques for maturation. Vineyards are planted in many parcels on a variety of terroirs in Terrasses de Larzac. (The size of the domain was reduced when Frédéric's partner, Victor Guizard, left in 2010 to form Domaine St. Sylvestre with his wife Sophie.) Blending is the focus here. "We vinify each cépage from each terrace in order to understand the terroir, but it takes 15 years, so as yet there aren't any single vineyard wines," Frédéric says. Montcalmès is planted with 60% Syrah, 20% Grenache, and 20% Mourvèdre; there is also a white (from a hectare divided between Roussanne and Marsanne). Wines are matured in 1- to 3-year-old barriques for two years, and bottled by the waning moon without filtration. The variety of terroirs provides Grenache varying from broad fleshiness to steely structure, and the house style is for a precise, harmonious elegance, very much a representation of the modern style of Languedoc. The red is labeled as Terrasses du Larzac, the white as Languedoc.

Château Pech Redon

Route Gruissan, Narbonne, 11100

(33) 04 68 90 41 22

chateaupechredon@wanadoo.fr

Christophe Bousquet

www.pech-redon.com

La Clape

La Clape, L'Epervier

30 ha; 50,000 bottles

Pech Redon is a truly unique location, on the site of an old Roman villa, several miles along a dirt track at the end of a large rocky plateau surrounded by impressive calcareous cliffs. The environment could not be more different from the seaside town of Narbonne, which is the official postal address. Christophe Bousquet bought the domain in 1988 upon the death of the previous owner, Jean Demolomben, a negociant in Narbonne. It's very isolated, but that was part of the appeal for Christophe. Regarded as a young Turk at the time, he is now one of the most established producers in the La Clape AOP. Pech Redon is at the highest point in La Clape (Pech Redon means "rounded peak.") Its elevation (about 200 m) makes it cooler and fresher than the rest of La Clape. All the wines are AOP La Clape (Christophe was much involved in its creation: he is president of the local producers' association). There is a classic Languedocian mix of the five black grape varieties (and also some whites). The terroir is relatively homogeneous, so differences between cuvées are due more to assemblage and élevage. The L'Epervier white cuvée is fresh and lively, but the main focus here is on the red cuvées, which ascend from Les Cades (8 months in cuve, fresh and lively, based on Syrah, Grenache, Cinsault, and Carignan), to L'Epervier (the flagship wine, 18 months in cuve, from Syrah, Grenache, Mourvèdre, and Carignan), and the weightiest, Centaurée (classic GSM, 24 months in oak fûts).

Domaine Peyre Rose

 Route Villeveyrac, Saint Pargoire, 34230

(33) 04 67 98 75 50

@ peyrerose@orange.fr

Marlène Soria

Languedoc

Coteaux du Languedoc, Clos des Cistes

23 ha; 32,000 bottles

To say that Peyre Rose is a bit tricky to find is an understatement. It's not easy to spot the entrance to the narrow unpaved track in Saint Pargoire that winds for several kilometers until it reaches the domain. "Follow the telegraph poles," the instructions say, but the faint of heart might well lose confidence along the way. It's entirely understandable that Marlène Soria used to come here on vacation for the savage quality of the countryside. She purchased 60 ha of garrigue, and then in 1970 planted some vines to make wine for personal consumption. The domain started later, with some plantings of Syrah in the 1980s, followed in 1985 by Mourvèdre and Grenache. Almost all of the plantings today are black varieties, with Syrah dominant, and just 3 ha of Rolle and Roussanne. This remains an intensely personal operation, with Marlène making the wines single-handed in the cave. Until 2002, everything was vinified in cuve, but since then about a quarter has been matured in foudres. Aging is quite extended here, with at least 7-8 years of élevage. A tasting at Peyre Rose in 2013 focused on current releases: 2003 and 2004. This is not your usual economic model. The wines move from the fleshy sex appeal of Marlène #3, to the more classic balance of Clos des Cistes (80% Syrah and 20% Grenache, the only wine really to show any restraint), and Clos Léone (80% Syrah and 20% Mourvèdre), but the general style is for intense, very ripe, exuberant fruits.

Domaine Olivier Pithon

2, carrer Tramontana 66600 Calce

(33) 04 68 38 50 21

pithon.olivier@wanadoo.fr

Olivier Pithon

www.domaineolivierpithon.com

IGP Côtes Catalanes

Côtes Catalanes, Le Clot

18 ha; 35,000 bottles

"My family were vignerons in the Loire, and I never thought of doing anything else," says Olivier Pithon. "After studying wine in other regions, I looked for vines, and I liked the varieties and area here at Calce." The winery entrance is a garage door in what looks like a residence in the main street of Calce, but inside is a small winemaking facility, crammed with equipment. Starting with 7 ha the first year, the domain has slowly expanded, and now includes white grapevines as well the original black. The vineyards are in the area that used to be the Vin de Pays Coteaux des Fenouillèdes (the name refers to the fennel that grows naturally on the hillsides), but they are all labeled as IGP Côtes de Catalanes. "The regulations for AOP are just too strict with regards to encépagement," Olivier says. There are three white cuvées and three red. The entry level wines, Mon P'tit Pithon, both red and white, come from purchased grapes: everything else comes from the estate. The top white wine, D18, is a blend of Grenache Gris and Blanc. The reds are the real heart of the domain, with Laïs based on a blend of Carignan and Grenache (it replaced two previous cuvées, La Coulée and Saturne); Le Pilou is a 100% Carignan from 100-year-old vines on calcareous terroir; and Le Clot (bottled only in magnums) is based on Grenache from schist. Olivier describes house style by saying, "The idea with the reds is to get elegance without aggressive tannins."

Prieuré Saint Jean de Bébian

Route de Nizas, 34120 Pézenas

(33) 04 67 98 13 60

info@bebian.com

Karen Turner

www.bebian.com

Languedoc

Languedoc, Le Prieuré

33 ha; 120,000 bottles

The winery sits on the site of a Roman villa, where perhaps vines were grown long ago, but the modern story starts with M. Roux, who sourced Syrah from Chave, Grenache from Château Rayas, Mourvèdre from Domaine Tempier, and Roussanne from Château Beaucastel. The estate was bought in 1994 by Chantal Lecouty and Jean-Claude Lebrun (formerly of the Revue du Vin). Karen Turner came as winemaker in 2004, and stayed on when the estate was sold to Russian owners in 2008. The top wine is labeled Grand Vin du Languedoc; the red has a high proportion of Syrah and Mourvèdre, and the white is more than half Roussanne. A second wine, La Chapelle de Bébian, is made in all three colors; the red is half Grenache, and the white is half Grenache Blanc. With more of an eye on the market, a new entry level line has been introduced under the name La Croix de Bébian. In addition, there is a Cabernet Sauvignon under the label L'Autre Versant. Even after some softening, the reds remain somewhat counter to the trend for instant gratification. "I have the impression that no one in Languedoc wants tannins any more, but I want them. One of the most important things about Bébian is that it's one of the few wines in Languedoc that ages well. It's probably best at 10-20 years after the vintage," Karen says. In my view, even La Chapelle isn't really ready after five years, and Prieuré does not open out until after ten years, making it one of the region's more ageworthy wines.

Château Puech Haut

📍 2250 route de Teyran, 34160 Saint Drézéry

📞 (33) 04 67 86 93 70

@ chateaupuech-haut@wanadoo.fr

👤 Alain Asselin

🌐 www.chateau-puech-haut.com

⬤ Languedoc

🍾 Languedoc St. Drézéry, Tête de Bélier

🚶 ⅏ G N

115 ha; 1,000,000 bottles

This is quite a grand estate, surrounded by vineyards, with a long drive flanked by olive trees. There's a spacious tasting room in a nineteenth century house, with a large barrel room on display just behind. But when Gérard Bru purchased the property in 1985, the land was mostly bare garrigue. There were 80 ha in the estate at the start, and then twenty years later this was increased to 200 ha, which makes it one of the larger properties in Languedoc. Most (100 ha) of vineyards are in Saint Drézéry (just northeast of Montpellier), but there are some additional plots in Pic St. Loup. Red, white, and rosé are produced in the entry level line, Prestige, and in the flagship line, Tête de Belier. The Prestige red is more than half Grenache; the Tête de Belier is three quarters Syrah, with smaller amounts of Grenache and Mourvèdre. There's also a Loup St. Pic red and occasional production of special cuvées. The style is full and powerful, with Châteauneuf-du-Pape as the model, to judge from the recent employment of Rhône oenologue Philippe Cambier as consultant. "Over the past four or five years the style has changed to be more Languedocian—warmer," says Alain Asselin in the tasting room. The whites have gone in a different direction. "Originally they were like all the others of the Languedoc—heavy," Alain says. The objective of a more mineral style for whites has been pursued by a Burgundian style of vinification, but they still show southern aromatics.

Domaine de La Rectorie

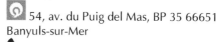

54, av. du Puig del Mas, BP 35 66651 Banyuls-sur-Mer

(33) 04 68 81 02 94

@ larectorie@wanadoo.fr

Jean-Emmanuel Parcé

www.la-rectorie.com

Banyuls

Collioure, Montagne

Banyuls, Cuvée Léon Parcé

30 ha; 80,000 bottles

Located in an old chapel in the center of Banyuls, this domain goes back to the start of the nineteenth century. Grapes were sent to the coop until 1984, when Marc and Thierry Parcé decided to produce their own wine. Today Thierry runs the domain together with his son Jean-Emmanuel, while Marc runs an associated negociant, Les Vins Parcé-Frères. Vineyards are scattered in small plots all around the steep hills of Banyuls. Plantings focus on Grenache. The sweet wines of Banyuls are only around 15% of production, with the main focus on dry red wines under the Collioure label. "It's often said that the wines of the south are too strong, too heavy, but we want to show they can have elegance," says Jean-Emmanuel. The red Collioure cuvées are L'Oriental (matured for a year in foudres, but with a modern impression), Côté Mer (matured in barriques and foudres, but fresh and approachable), and Montagne (the most complex assemblage and the most elegant impression, with the least Grenache, matured in barriques and foudres for 18 months). Under the Banyuls label there are three cuvées of fortified wines: Thérèse Reig comes from an early harvest, with sweet, ripe, black fruits; Léon Parcé is harvested later from select parcels and has an intriguing mix of savory and sweet influences; and the new cuvée, Pierre Rapidol, is matured for six years before release to show an intense, oxidized style. Under the IGP Côte Vermeille there is a dry Rancio wine, the Pedro Soler cuvée.

Domaine Le Roc des Anges **

LE
ROC DES
DOMAINE
ANGES

SEGNA DE COR

2 0 0 8

CÔTES DU
ROUSSILLON VILLAGES
MARJORIE & STEPHANE GALLET
VIGNERONS A 66720 MONTNER

2 Place de l'Aire, 66720 Montner

(33) 04 68 29 16 62

ocdesanges@wanadoo.fr

Marjorie Gallet

www.rocdesanges.com

Côtes du Roussillon Villages

IGP Catalanes, Vignes Centenaires Carignan

28 ha; 60,000 bottles

Coming from the northern Rhône after working at Yves Cuilleron and Pierre Gaillard, Marjorie Gallet cut short an apprenticeship at Domaine Gauby when the chance came to purchase her own vineyards in 2001. Roc des Anges started with 10 ha. Vineyards are around Montner, a village in the Agly valley in the far south of Roussillon. Originally located at Tautavel, a new cave was built at Montner in 2008, and her husband Stéphane came from nearby Mas Amiel to join Marjorie. (The name Montner derives from Monte Negro, reflecting the dark color of the schist; this was part of the Vin de Pays Coteaux Fenouillèdes before it was abolished.) The focus is on traditional Mediterranean varieties (Carignan, Grenache, and Macabeo, supplemented by a little Syrah). Plantings are about two thirds black to one third white. Wines are matured in a mixture of concrete and old wood. Most whites are IGP Pyrénées Orientales, with Iglesia Vella coming from pure Grenache Gris, and the Vieilles Vignes coming from 70-year-old vines, mostly Grenache Gris. L'Oca Blanc comes from Macabeo. Most reds are AOP Côtes du Roussillon Villages. Segna de Cor comes from young vines; the Vieilles Vignes is a blend from old Grenache and Carignan (vines over seventy years old) plus some younger Syrah; and Vignes Centenaires Carignan cones from 3 ha of very old Carignan. There are also IGP des Côtes Catalanes in both red and white, as well as a rosé and passerillé dessert wine.

Château Rouquette Sur Mer

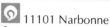 11101 Narbonne

(33) 04 68 49 90 41

 bureau@chateaurouquette.com

 Jacques Boscary

www.chateaurouquette.com

La Clape

La Clape, Clos de la Tour

55 ha; 200,000 bottles

Faithful to its name, Château Rouquette sur Mer is on the sea, overlooking Narbonne Plage. A family domain since the 1940s, this is a large estate; vineyards surround the property and run down towards the sea, but altogether around 50 separate parcels are scattered all over La Clape, making for significant heterogeneity in the soils. Château Rouquette is definitely on the oenotourism circuit, with a professional tasting room open almost every day, and a constant stream of visitors, many bringing their own containers to be filled with one of the three colors right out of the spigot in the tasting room. There are wines at all levels from Vin de France to IGP to AOP, with the range extending all the way from the bulk wines to special cuvées. It would be easy to be put off by the touristic atmosphere in the tasting room, but the special cuvées are in fact the antithesis of the bulk wine, with something of a concentration on Mourvèdre, which is a minor component in Cuvée Henry Lapierre (matured in new barriques), but is three quarters of Clos de la Tour. The top wine is Cuvée Absolute, where only 2,000 bottles are produced from a selection of the best lots, with the parcels and varieties changing each year, but Mourvèdre was always dominant in my tastings. The wide range makes it hard to define house style here, but at the level of cuvées, the animal quality of Mourvèdre stands out. A dessert wine, Vendanges d'Automne, is made from late harvest Bourboulenc in some years.

Château La Tour Boisée

11800 Laure-Minervois

(33) 04 68 78 10 04

info@domainelatourboisee.com

Jean-Louis Poudou

www.domainelatourboisee.com

Minervois

Minervois, Marie-Claude

85 ha; 300,000 bottles

This old family domain dates from 1826. A person of strong opinions ("AOC says something—it is controlled—but AOP is nothing, it is a trick to talk about Protégé"), current proprietor Jean-Louis Poitou, who took over in 1982, tries to maintain tradition, growing 17 grape varieties in his many parcels. "We can take a Burgundian approach and identify a place for each variety," he says. He's been trying to reintroduce some of the old Gris varieties that used to be grown in the area. About 70% of production is red, with the rest divided between white and rosé; 60% of the wines are Minervois; the others, including monovarietals and some unusual combinations of varieties, are in one of the local IGPs. The difference is due more to the regulations of the AOPs and IGPs than quality. "Our IGP wines are worked in the same spirit as AOP with similar yields, 40 hl/ha for the IGP, and 30 hl/ha for the AOP." The whites of Minervois are blends of the usual southern varieties, but the IGP Coteaux de Peyriac is a Chardonnay. There's a range of red monovarietals in the IGP, but the most interesting wine here is the red Minervois Marie-Claude, a blend of Syrah, Grenache, and Carignan. A late harvest wine from Marsanne, Minervois Noble, has some botrytis as well as passerillage, and matures for ten years in old tonneaux. In addition to the wines that are labeled as Château Tour Boisée, there's also an entry level line (including red, white, and rosé) under the label of Domaine Tour Boisée.

Château de La Tuilerie

Route de Saint Gilles, 30900 Nîmes

(33) 04 66 70 07 52

vins@chateautuilerie.com

Chantal et Pierre-Yves Comte

www.chateautuilerie.com

Costières de Nîmes

Costières de Nîmes, Eole

66 ha; 400,000 bottles

Located just outside Nîmes, which has changed its allegiance from Languedoc to Rhône, Château de la Tuilerie has a foot in both camps, as it produces both AOP Costières de Nîmes and IGP d'Oc. Purchased by Chantale Comte's father in 1955, it's been a leader in improving quality in Costières de Nîmes. "When I started thirty years ago, the region made vins de café, more like Beaujolais. I could see that if we waited with harvest—they were harvesting green berries—you could make great wine. There were no barriques in Costières, we were the first," Chantale says. In both AOP and IGP, Château de la Tuilerie has entry level wines (the Château wine for AOP and Celebration for IGP) and higher level wines (Eole for AOP and Alma Soror for IGP). The vineyards are in fact almost all in the Costières de Nîmes, except for some tiny plots in the IGP. They are on the oldest soils of the appellation, rather poor with lots of pebbles. The IGP line is extended with some varieties that aren't allowed in the AOP, but the focus in reds is on Syrah. "I have tried to make wines in the spirit of the Rhône, especially the Syrah of the northern Rhône," Chantale says. I find the whites—which are barrel-fermented in new oak—to be generally more interesting than the reds; the Eole white (a blend of many varieties) is rich but fresh, with a real density and texture supporting good development with age. The château also produces olive oil, and rums from a property on Martinique.

Index of Estates by Rating

Alphabetical Index of Estates

INTELLIGENT GUIDES TO WINES & TOP VINEYARDS

WINES OF FRANCE SERIES

1 *Bordeaux*

2 *Southwest France*

3 *Burgundy: Chablis & Côte d'Or*

4 *Southern Burgundy, Beaujolais & Jura*

5 *Champagne*

6 *Alsace*

7 *The Loire*

8 *The Rhône*

9 *Languedoc*

10 *Provence and Corsica*

WINE OF EUROPE SERIES

11 *Barolo & Barbaresco*

12 *Tuscany (coming soon)*

13 *Port & the Douro*

NEW WORLD WINE SERIES

14 *Napa Valley & Sonoma*

BOOKS by Benjamin Lewin MW

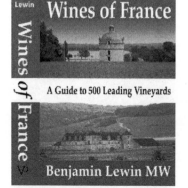

Wines of France

This comprehensive account of the vineyards and wines of France today is extensively illustrated with photographs and maps of each wine-producing area. Leading vineyards and winemakers are profiled in detail, with suggestions for wines to try and vineyards to visit.

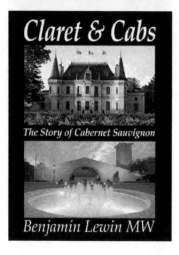

*Claret & Cabs:
the Story of Cabernet Sauvignon*

This worldwide survey of Cabernet Sauvignon and its blends extends from Bordeaux through the New World, defines the character of the wine from each region, and profiles leading producers.

In Search of Pinot Noir

Pinot Noir is a uniquely challenging grape with an unrivalled ability to reflect the character of the site where it grows. This world wide survey of everywhere Pinot Noir is grown extends from Burgundy to the New World, and profiles leading producers.

Wine Myths and Reality

Extensively illustrated with photographs, maps, and charts, this behind-the-scenes view of winemaking reveals the truth about what goes into a bottle of wine. Its approachable and entertaining style immediately engages the reader in the wine universe.

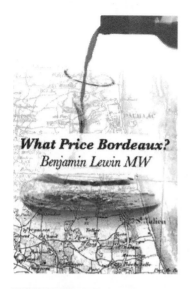

What Price Bordeaux?

A revolution is underway in Bordeaux. Top chateaux have been obtaining unprecedented prices for their wines, while smaller chateaux are going bankrupt. Extending from the changing character of Bordeaux wines to market forces, this unique overview reveals the forces making Bordeaux wine what it is today.

About the Author

Benjamin Lewin MW brings a unique combination of qualifications in wine and science to bear on the world of wine. He is one of only 300 Masters of Wine, and was the founding Editor of *Cell* journal. His previous books received worldwide critical acclaim for their innovative approach. Lewin also writes the myths and realities column in the *World of Fine Wine*, and contributes to *Decanter* magazine, *Wine & Spirits*, among others. His blog on wine is at *www.lewinonwine.com*. He divides his time between the eastern United States and the wine-growing regions of Europe, and is presently working on his next book.

39278603R00049

Made in the USA
Middletown, DE
10 January 2017